Richard Unsworth is a leading garden designer and is Garden Editor and a contributing writer for *Belle* magazine. He is also the owner of Sydney's renowned outdoor store, Garden Life.

Having grown up surrounded by nature in the north of England, Richard inherited a love of gardening from his parents, and, from an early age, started earning pocket money by working in the gardens of his family, friends and neighbours.

After he moved to Sydney over twenty years ago he furthered his love of urban horticulture with formal study, and started his first business, Apartment Garden Living, focusing on inner-city garden design.

In 2001 he opened his first store, Garden Life, in Sydney's Darlinghurst. There he continued to hone his natural talent for design and widened his design practice to work in larger spaces both in the city and further afield. In 2008 Garden Life moved to larger premises in Redfern.

Richard's love of travel and adventure takes him to places far and wide to find inspiration as he discovers new and old wares. Garden Life is a celebration of natural, unique and contemporary pieces and plants sourced both globally and locally.

In addition to running the business, Richard is a founding member of the James Street Reserve Community Garden, located in the lane behind the Garden Life store.

Garden Life

—

Richard Unsworth

Photography by
Nicholas Watt

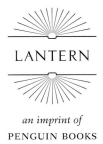

LANTERN

an imprint of
PENGUIN BOOKS

Contents

—

Introduction 1

PART 1

Create

CHAPTER 1: Large Spaces 10

CHAPTER 2: Small Spaces 90

PART 2

Connect

CHAPTER 3: Harvest 130

CHAPTER 4: Share 150

PART 3

Cultivate

CHAPTER 5: People 172

CHAPTER 6: Discovery 186

Final thoughts 211

Acknowledgements 213

Index 215

Introduction

I run a business called Garden Life, which is a combination of retail and garden design. The retail side is a lot of fun, and I love to fill the store with beautiful pots and other objects which I have sourced from my travels. Garden design is the backbone of the business though, where I started and where I get to flex my creative muscle. I am passionate about helping people transform their urban outdoor environments – their own patch of green space, their retreat, and the place where they can connect with others. I see our role as garden designers as, quite simply, to help our clients create the outdoor space they want to be in. Although practical issues and aesthetics are important, it's more important to get the feeling of the garden right. It is more important to me, as a designer, to understand how a client wants a space to feel, than how he or she wants it to look. Of course, some clients just want it to look great, and that's fine, too.

Some of our clients are pretty vague about what they want, and others come armed to the teeth with clippings, scrapbooks, journals and lists. I'm not too fussed whether it's one or the other, or anything in between. As long as we can get into their heads and try to understand their expectations and desires, then we can work with them to create their personal outdoor space. My aim is simple – I want our clients to be able to just sit and be in the space, alone or with others, to be at ease and feel like they belong. If we can achieve this, then I feel we have succeeded.

Garden aesthetics are of course heavily influenced by fixed factors such as the location, the local environment, the architecture of the home and the client's lifestyle. More than ever before, we live now with a connection to the outdoors through contemporary architecture, and this inside/outside relationship is in everybody's consciousness.

To create a successful garden, you need to find the right balance between planting and the built form, with neither one dominating the other. So many designs concentrate solely on the built form, with scant attention to the planting and vice versa – careful consideration of both is critical.

It's important not to take a 'cookie cutter' approach to garden design. Every space is different, and every client has different needs and aspirations, so we try to approach each project with fresh eyes. Plants must be used in the conditions they favour; placing plants in the wrong position is the most common mistake people make. I do have some favourites – the ones that have proved themselves to be reliable performers over the years. I try to integrate imaginative, fresh planting with

a core of proven performers to keep things fresh and ensure our planting schemes last the distance.

Most of my inspiration comes from the great outdoors. I grew up amongst the limestone walls and rugged slopes of the Yorkshire Dales. Here in Australia I love the energy of the whole landscape – the bush and the countryside, the hills and the valleys, the changing colours of the outback desert or a rocky cliff-top escarpment. I love the movement of native grasses and the gnarly, barked forms of angophoras and banksias. I am inspired by walking through deciduous woodlands, seeing bluebells in spring and claret leaves in autumn, and I love bushwalking close to my place in the Blue Mountains.

Australian garden designer Annie Wilkes has been a major influence – I learnt so much about composition and scale whilst working for her at Parterre Gardens. I'm also a big fan of Hugh Main and Myles Baldwin, who both have highly original styles. Overseas, the dreamy French gardens of Nicole de Vesian are works of art; American landscape architect Andrea Cochran always pushes the boundaries with her geometric layouts, and UK-based Italian designer Luciano Giubbilei creates very chic gardens in tight urban spaces.

Australian landscape designer Rick Eckersley once told me that he sees his job as 'being a conduit for his clients' desires and ideas', and I think that's exactly where good garden design starts. We have to channel our clients' dreams into creating something achievable, given their space, budget and other individual factors. I always try to be aware that it's my client's garden, not mine, whatever I'm doing – whether it's opening up expansive views or screening unsightly elements; composing intimate spaces or styling areas to focus attention and create drama. It's all about creating a sense of belonging and connection for the clients, their friends and family when they are in the space.

ABOVE Nicole de Vesian's dreamy La Louve garden in Provence.

A Bit About Me

Both my parents were keen hobby gardeners (my Mum's garden is a big part of her life, and she is still getting stuck into it at seventy-six) and I was lucky to grow up in a lovely home in Yorkshire surrounded by a large, rambling garden. The semi-formal grounds required constant maintenance and, as part of our pocket money conditions, my brother, sisters and I all had to help out.

We had a traditional A-frame greenhouse attached to the garage at the end of the drive where Dad loved to grow tomatoes, zucchini and other vegies. It was there that he taught me how to grow my very first crop – radishes. Mum was the queen of fruit-growing, and each summer we had bountiful crops of strawberries, raspberries, gooseberries and a fine clump of rhubarb.

Looking back, I think I was destined to have my own store, as I have always loved selling things. When I was fourteen, I got my first job at my uncle's hardware store, where I had my first experience of merchandising and display – there wasn't much I couldn't do with a sink plunger, some brass hinges and some sticky-backed plastic!

Aged seventeen, I advertised my gardening services in the local newspaper and, before I knew it, had cornered the market in gardens for geriatric ladies. I also tried my hand at golf course design, building a putting green behind a local pub. That was my first foray into laying turf, and I loved the instant gratification of it.

After I left school, I worked in an upmarket local nursery, where I enjoyed the mixture of horticulture and retail, then in the early '90s I decided to set off and try my luck in Australia.

I quickly fell in love with Australia's vibrancy and freshness – so evident in the people, the climate and, especially, the landscape.

I started a three-year horticulture course at Ryde TAFE which gave me a good grounding in the fundamentals of professional gardening. We had a wonderful soil teacher called Judy Fakes, whose passion for the brown stuff was completely infectious, and, by the end of the course, I felt the same way. Over the years I have noticed that most soil problems disappear with the addition of generous amounts of composted poo from one animal or another.

While I was studying I worked for Annie Wilkes and Richard Haigh, managing one of their Parterre stores. Annie was a whirlwind of energy, with a passion for creating formal, French-inspired gardens. Every other week or so, she would

ABOVE LEFT Laying turf in my sister Kathy's back garden in London, 1986.

ABOVE RIGHT The Royal Botanic Garden Edinburgh, circa 1990 – pretending to be a gardener!

breeze into the store and we would set about restyling the space – she taught me composition and styling, and helped train my eye to see how different objects worked together (or not).

After I left Parterre I bought a van and some tools and started doing some gardening work. I had been doing some work for the lovely Saskia Havekes at her shop Grandiflora in Potts Point and through her and other word of mouth, I started to get some small garden design gigs.

Soon I decided to spread my wings and start my own business. At the time, just before the Sydney Olympics in 2000, there was an explosion in apartment-building, and I soon realised there was a gap in the market for gardening in small urban spaces. My first business, Apartment Garden Living, was born.

I got my big break when *The Sydney Morning Herald's* Domain featured a piece on small-space gardening, and put me on its cover. That led to lots of enquiries from people moving from suburban homes with sprawling gardens into small apartments with confined outdoor areas.

Clients, I found, were often perplexed about how best to approach a balcony, rooftop or terrace. I would often arrive at the first consultation to see a pair of dead topiaries, a citrus tree full of scale in a shady spot, or some sick-looking gardenias. People downsizing from larger properties were transporting their favourite plant specimens from sheltered gardens to exposed, windy rooftops where they were being shredded to bits.

We developed a reputation for being good gardeners in these small urban spaces, and I found the work really satisfying, because the transformation was instant, and people loved it. They left for work in the morning looking at a bare concrete area, and returned to find a living, breathing, mature garden.

As the business started to grow, I employed other horticulturists, giving me time to see clients and look for more work, and soon I began to take on some larger projects, which was incredibly exciting.

ABOVE The store.

PART 1

Create

Large Spaces 10

Small Spaces 90

The American landscape architect Steve Martino once told me he saw his job as like that of a set designer – 'editing the landscape like crazy', and I can relate to that.

Every dwelling, whatever its size and style, needs the right garden to ground and frame it. A well-designed and considered outdoor space will transform your home.

Sometimes my work involves creating a whole new garden, other times I am asked to renovate what's already there. Each has its own challenges and rewards. When you are creating a garden from scratch you have complete freedom, a blank canvas on which to build the new landscape. It's an opportunity to enhance the architecture, bed the house in and tick all the boxes on the client's wishlist. Rejuvenating an existing garden is different but just as enjoyable; I love the challenge of revitalising and updating tired and neglected spaces, taking them to the next level.

The first thing I do when we start a new project is to take an inventory of the existing garden assets, so that I can work out what is worth keeping and what needs to go. Once I know that, I can focus on what is coming out, and this is the part I really love. There is something about getting stuck into a garden and removing everything that isn't working – the unwanted plants, the dead foliage, or the bad paving. It's like a metaphor for life – it is very liberating to rid ourselves of the things that aren't working for us, cleaning out the dead wood, and leaving a clear canvas on which to create a new beginning.

The results can be quite immediate, although I hesitate to use the word 'makeover', as this suggests a temporary fix – a quick garish touch-up for a brief period of pleasure or a house sale.

One thing it's important to remember, as you embark upon creating a new outdoor space, is that every garden (provided it is well-planned) looks best as it matures. Plants grow into and take ownership of their space, and, provided their food, water and nurturing needs are being met, keep on giving back and performing. So don't expect too much, too soon!

I have worked in large spaces and small, and what follows is a selection of some of my favourites. Some were completely new builds, some were garden renovation, and some were a mixture of the two.

CHAPTER 1

Large Spaces

It's exciting and challenging to be involved in larger scale design projects.

Having more space allows us to develop fully all the elements required for a successful landscape. We also have more opportunity to create a sense of journey and discovery within the garden.

We can use larger plants with bigger impact and can develop complex planting schemes with more depth and nuance. The greater landscape – whether it be ocean, harbour or surrounding paddocks – can work as a backdrop, providing a setting for the larger garden.

Whilst it's always important to focus on the bigger picture, we often approach large spaces as if they were a series of smaller spaces – each area must be able to stand alone.

There are so many different kinds of large garden – here I look at two formal gardens, a relaxed garden, a coastal garden and a garden made up of pots and planters, and give you some ideas on how you might want to create a garden like that for yourself.

A Formal Garden

POINT PIPER

I think of myself as very lucky with my clients. I have good relationships with all of them, and some of those relationships have blossomed into close friendships. That's how it is with the owners of this magnificent home at Point Piper. I first met them when they were renting a property we looked after and a year or two later they called us in to help with the garden of their new home. We have now worked together on six different properties.

This was the fifth project I worked on with them, and this ongoing relationship, plus my intimate knowledge of their sense of style, ensured there was a good degree of trust on their part and a strong desire on mine to push the boundaries. I knew how much they loved their new house, and working with them to create a beautiful garden was part of helping them to feel at home there. Whilst neither of them are gardeners, they are purveyors of beauty and big fans of the Mediterranean culture and landscape. They wanted a garden that matched the impressive formal architecture of the house. There had to be elements of grandeur, and some big, bold statements, as well as some softness in certain areas.

This magnificent home sits right in the middle of the dress circle in Sydney Harbour, and when I first saw it the view took my breath away. Okay, so it wasn't just the view – the house itself is really quite something. Designed by Michael Suttor, this Italianate mansion occupies two blocks and comprises five levels, with the gardens starting at street level then cascading down to the water. The proportions are grand, with vaulted ceilings, sweeping stairs, huge doors and fine, classical architectural detailing everywhere. The living areas on the ground floor lead into a central cobbled courtyard, and the house opens up at the back onto a large terrace facing the view.

The house hadn't been lived in for some time, and although its interior was in good condition, the outside was another matter. The gardens were seriously letting the house down. Thankfully, the architect had given a lot of thought to the structural layout, and there was a great sense of scale and proportion, so the bones of the garden were already there. However, most of the planting was dull, uninspired and completely overgrown. There were boring, shrubby plants everywhere, scrappy climbers covering beautiful sandstone walls, and groundcovers rambling unchecked and merging into other plants. A large conifer boundary hedge screened the neighbouring house on one side, and there were some lower plantings of **BOX** and **LILLYPILLY** hedges that were well-established, but in poor health and extremely

Star jasmine frames the picture-perfect view.

On the left is an Italian terracotta urn planted with bromeliads, next to a spartan juniper conifer and elephant ears (you can see where they get their name!), all surrounded by low box Japanese hedge.

The owners' beloved Wollemi pines frame the steps down to the pool, one of our Turkish urns nestles in the background, and the *Convolvulus sabatius* 'Two Moons' creeps over the sandstone walls, softening them.

woolly. I was itching to get my hands on the garden, which needed some serious work to bring it up to scratch.

Whilst the house demanded formal surroundings, the last thing I wanted to do was to create a clichéd, stuffy formal garden. What I wanted was to breathe some life back into the property, and to create a fresh, classic, pared-back look that had some delicate, light and fun aspects to it.

First, I had to decide what to keep from the existing garden. We ended up keeping only the large, conifer hedges, which provided privacy on the boundary, the existing **LILLYPILLY** and the smaller **BOX HEDGES** which swept around the lawn. They all needed a firm clipping and pruning, and the soil was badly in need of nourishment. We added cow manure, Dynamic Lifter (chicken poo, deadly smelly but great for foliage growth) and a slow-release fertiliser to improve soil health.

THE STEPS DOWN TO THE POOL AREA

At the top of the stairs, leading down to the pool, we replaced a pair of rather twee **LILLYPILLY** topiaries with a majestic pair of **WOLLEMI PINES** (*Wollemia nobilis*), which had travelled with the owners from their previous home. They are dearly loved, as the plants are grown from cuttings taken from ancient trees in the Wollemi National Park, north-west of Sydney. We will need to keep our eye on their size, and they might need some pruning as they can grow rather large, but they look magnificent and natural at the top of the steps.

The house came with a pair of huge, ornate Italianate urns, one of which stands midway between the pool and the lawn, and the other up on the lawn. Whilst the style and size were appropriate for the house, the faux sandstone colour was very wrong. I hate anything fake, and that includes something trying to look like sandstone when it's not! We decided to make them darker and more dramatic, and came up with the idea of repainting them with Murobond Bridge Paint to give a luxe industrial, metallic feel. The paint has iron filings in it that catch the light and it's used on the Harbour Bridge, hence the name bridge paint. We massed both urns with the succulent **DONKEY TAIL** (*Sedum morganianum*)*,* which trailed down and softened the sides, and now they are amongst my favourite features of the garden.

We didn't change the planting much at the pool level; it was more a case of fixing what was already there. The **CREEPING FIG** (*Ficus pumila*) was growing out of control on the sandstone boulders between the pool and lawn levels, so we cropped it back hard to follow the exact contour of the rock underneath, softly enveloping it like some verdant artwork by Christo and Jeanne-Claude. We then added a pair of old, Turkish planters at the bottom of the steps, planted with architectural foliage to contrast with the clipped **FIG**.

THE LAWN

This is really the meaty part of the garden – our main opportunity to make an impact. The first task was to remove everything, apart from the large, conifer hedges and the smaller, mature **BOX** and **LILLYPILLY** hedges. For texture and colour contrast, we planted advanced specimens of **EVERGREEN MAGNOLIAS** (*Magnolia grandiflora* 'Little Gem') and large **SPEAR LILY** (*Doryanthes palmeri*). Smaller plantings included clumps of **BEARDED IRIS** (*Iris germanica*), clipped balls of the silver-foliaged **SHRUB GERMANDER** (*Teucrium fruticans*) and drifts of the dark-foliaged *Euphorbia* 'Black Bird'. We mass-planted *Convolvulus sabatius* 'Two Moons', which are now starting to trail over and soften the sandstone retaining walls facing the harbour. Most of the flowers are white, but then they throw out some random blue ones – hence their cultivar name, 'Two Moons'.

TOP LEFT A harbourside pool lies at the bottom of the five-level garden.

TOP RIGHT Massive donkey tail sedum pours out of the top of an Italianate urn which we transformed with Murobond Bridge Paint – so-called because it's used on the Harbour Bridge.

BOTTOM We cropped the creeping fig hard so that it enveloped the sandstone boulders surrounding the pool.

FOLLOWING PAGE Lawn surrounded by double hedge of Japanese box and lillypilly.

THE COURTYARD

The central courtyard is integral to the living areas of the house and, whilst the cobbled flooring and terracotta tiled roof are lovely details, it all looked very bare and empty when my clients first moved in. The architecture dominated, and it all needed softening. We planted four striated urns with large specimens of **JAPANESE MAPLE** (*Acer palmatum*), the gentle, deep-bronze foliage sitting in each corner of the courtyard, and we placed smaller striated pots massed with **CAST-IRON PLANT** (*Aspidistra elatior*) on either side of the huge front door.

To give the courtyard further character, we composed a table with some interesting antique objects, including a collection of small pots planted with various succulents including **JADE, ECHEVERIA** and **COTYLEDON**. One of the key pieces is an old brass ornament I found in Sri Lanka, and it sits perfectly at the back, adding some old world bling.

Our clients are happy with the results. She works long hours and uses the garden for relaxation and exercise, often doing her lunges on the lawn. Her favourite aspect of the house is the view from down at the pool level looking back up. She told me, 'I look at the house from the water and just love the different shapes and textures in the garden, the way the fig grows over the sandstone. The garden provides a beautiful softness to the house.' He travels a lot for work, and loves to come and just sit on the timber seat we placed for him in the garden to help wind down and recover from his jet lag.

Because we maintain the garden weekly, it always looks its best, and I love seeing the space mature. My clients' desire to invest in, update and transform the garden, together with the fact that they are sticklers for perfection, has ensured that this magnificent house now has the garden it deserves.

TOP LEFT Massed cast-iron plants in striated urns frame the entry to the courtyard.

TOP RIGHT The courtyard features a marble table with a composition of succulents massed in antique pots.

CENTRE LEFT Different textures complement each other.

BOTTOM LEFT Another simple but striking composition.

BOTTOM RIGHT I like to mix things up a bit – here a rounded stone pot contrasts with a spiky agave.

I love to use different varieties of finishes and forms - the centrepiece here is an old Sri Lankan ornament, and the whole composition is beautifully framed by star jasmine in full flower.

On the steps leading down to the swimming pool clipped balls of shrub germander on the right contrast nicely with the sword-like leaves of the bearded iris and Gymea lily. You can see the majestic Wollemi pines on either side of the stairs.

Star jasmine does a great job of softening the house. It will grow wherever you put support.

Japanese yew in old French Anduze pots.

Graceful kentia palm foliage.

Wollemi pine foliage.

The low hedge of Japanese box encircles the lawn.

A lillypilly hedge sits underneath the box hedge, separated by the sandstone capping.

- We inherited the advanced hedges of 'Leighton Green' conifer hedge.
- Evergreen magnolia with its huge white flowers is a classic choice.
- Sword-like leaves of Gymea lily look striking next to clipped, tight foliage.
- Clipped balls of shrub germander with their silver foliage provide a nice contrast.
- A pair of Wollemi pines sits at the top of the steps down to the pool.
- Convolvulus softens the walls.
- Antique Turkish Enez pot.

Another Formal Garden

BELLEVUE HILL

—

Okay, so there's not too many houses around with a driveway measuring almost 1000 square metres. This is a great example of how to create a formal entrance and a great sense of arrival.

The original house was quite ugly, with a colourful past. It is rumoured that, before my clients bought (and virtually rebuilt) it, there was many a gentleman visiting at all hours of the day for, shall we say, 'relaxation' purposes. My clients wanted to create a home that was formal and classic, with a garden to match. My brief was to create a truly exceptional, formal garden which would provide a foundation upon which the new house would shine.

I had worked on the garden in their previous home so I knew instinctively what they wanted; my aim was to take that further and surprise them. It would have been easy to create a standard formal garden using the traditional palette of plants, but I wanted to introduce some sexier, less conventional elements that would really create a 'wow' factor.

When I first saw the driveway, it was a rambling mess of overgrown grass and weeds, with very few redeeming features. One big plus was a smattering of good, mature trees and a majestic clump of palms at the top. The front garden, which housed a tennis court, consisted of small patches of weed-filled grass and some fake plastic palms in plastic pots. There was no real back garden, just an unattractive pool enclosure. It all had to go; we needed to develop a new scheme for the whole garden. Because the driveway was roughly the same size as the combined area of the house and surrounding gardens, the challenge was to make the rest of the grounds as impressive as it was going to be.

I wanted the driveway to create a sense of anticipation and intrigue, providing a grand entry to the newly built house. The key to its success was going to be strong symmetry of the layout, planting and features. It was also important for the garden to look good as you were sitting in a car driving up the driveway. To help define the garden beds on either side of the drive and to provide much needed structure, we created a series of low terrace walls, using sandstone reclaimed from the original house. When viewed from the bottom of the drive, the new beds created by these horizontal walls had the effect of widening the space, and we started to see a strong form emerging.

Next, we needed to find a solution for the concrete surface. My clients wanted to repave the entire length, but I didn't think that was necessary, and looked for

Looking down the driveway to the front gates. Clumps of palms frame the top of the driveway, and a low hedge of Japanese box surrounds beds of contrasting foliage.

other options that would give us a smarter appearance without the cost. We settled on resurfacing with an epoxy polymer-based product. The darker colour made a huge difference to the space, smartening it up at a fraction of the cost of repaving. Up towards the house, where we wanted a finer, more detailed finish, we settled on hand-cut walnut travertine laid in a herringbone pattern, providing a soft, weathered and wonderfully detailed surface.

We quickly spent the money we had saved on resurfacing the driveway on a large pair of cast bronze striated urns, which we placed in rectangular ponds halfway up the drive, and plumbed so that water could be pumped up the middle and flow down the sides. We softened the pond edges with a mass of purple flowering **PLECTRANTHUS** (*Plectranthus ciliatus*). We placed two pairs of large, contemporary charcoal bowls above and below the ponds on either side. The crisp, fresh shapes of the planters prevent the driveway from looking too rigid, and we planted them with advanced specimens of **CYCADS** (*Cycas revoluta*) under-planted with **SWEET VIOLET** (*Viola odorata*).

For the driveway beds we developed a central grouping of architectural feature plants with a contrasting lower layer, all encased in a border of low **JAPANESE BOX** (*Buxus microphylla* var. *japonicus*). Good old box hedge. I wanted to avoid using it on this job as it's such a clichéd, overused plant in Sydney's Eastern suburbs, but it really is the best plant for a crisp, reliable low hedge. Within the box hedge we used contrasting and architectural foliage to sex up the scheme and create interest. We surrounded large clumps of bronzed-leaf **BROMELIAD** (*Alcantarea imperials* 'Rubra') with the perennially performing **GIANT MONDO GRASS** (*Ophiopogon jaburan*) and mixed the long, sword-shaped leaves of **GYMEA LILY** (*Doryanthes excelsa*) with the softer, silvery-grey **NEW ZEALAND ROCK LILY** (*Arthropodium cirratum*). Lower down the driveway, massed **MEXICAN LILY** (*Beschorneria yuccoides*) created a strong entry down by the impressive new front gates. Further up towards the house, on the boundary, we planted the textured conifer **CHINESE JUNIPER** (*Juniperus chinensis* 'Kaizuka') which provided a more interesting screen than a conifer hedge.

The front garden is fairly small, so we had to make sure that what we planted here had impact and performed well. The hard structure of the house, tennis court and top of the driveway needed softening, so we planted a pair of **BLACK TUPELO** (*Nyssa sylvatica*), a soft-leafed, medium-sized deciduous tree with horizontal branches, to provide scale against the bulk of the house. We also planted smart hedges of **VIBURNUM** (*Viburnum odoratissimum*) and groupings of **GYMEA LILY** and **CYCADS**, providing a lovely deep green colour contrast with the stone-coloured house.

Around the perimeter of the garden beds we continued the theme of structured hedges with contrasting foliage and form. Mass plantings of **COMMON JADE** (*Crassula ovata*) softened the borders of the tennis court and upper drive, creating a wonderfully organic, low, border hedge. Immediately behind this, we planted the silver-foliaged **BUSH GERMANDER** (*Teucrium fruticans*) to provide a strong, slickly clipped contrast.

Inside the beds we placed over-scaled antique olive jars from Turkey, more clumps of **GYMEA LILY** and **WHITE FLOWERING SAGE** (*Salvia leucantha* 'Velour White') giving a soft yet structured Mediterranean feel.

We placed a large pair of **OLIVES** (*Olea europea*) at the entry to the porte-cochere, and we designed a traditional water feature to add interest at the main entry, using three cast bronze spouts and an antique mirror. That was actually our second attempt at creating the focal point. We had originally installed some handmade, bottle green fish-scale tiles but just as we had almost finished tiling the back wall, the client decided she absolutely HATED it! That's all part of the process – the main

TOP One side of the driveway entry, in front of the new gates, where we mass-planted Mexican lily under a black tupelo to provide definition, and layered jade hedge and box hedge under the lily to frame it all. This composition is mirrored on the other side.

BOTTOM LEFT One of four large charcoal bowls planted with cycads framing the rectangular ponds seen on page 34.

CENTRE RIGHT A Gymea lily provides architectural foliage.

BOTTOM RIGHT White sage planted in between two Turkish urns.

THIS PAGE We used a pair of cast bronze striated urns in rectangular ponds halfway up the driveway to create a strong focal point, and mass-planted plectranthrus to soften the sides.

OPPOSITE Water features and specimen planting are big features in this garden.

thing to remember is that it's not our garden – it's our clients who will be looking at it every day, not us.

The back garden area surrounding the pool was quite confined, so we didn't have much space to play with. We softened the house walls, which were quite close to the pool, with the deciduous creeper **BOSTON IVY** (*Parthenocissus tricuspidata*). It's such a great climber, adding instant age and a feeling that the newly built house had been there for decades. For privacy we planted another hedge of **CHINESE JUNIPER** (*Juniperus chinensis* 'Kaizuka') in the back boundary beds. In front of this we layered various types of foliage to make the most of the narrow beds and create a feeling of depth.

We used a neat, formal low hedge of **JAPANESE BOX** at the front of the raised beds to enclose and define silver-clipped balls of **BUSH GERMANDER** (*Teucrium fruticans*), spring-flowering **INDIAN HAWTHORN** (*Rhaphiolepis indica* 'Snow Maiden'), grey-green **PERSIAN SHIELD** (*Strobilanthes gossypinus*) and purple-bronzed leaves of *Billbergia* 'Hallelujah', a type of bromeliad. We introduced some rough texture and fresher stand-out planting with some lovely rustic Turkish **DAGAR** planters, potted with variegated *Agave americana* 'Mediopicta Alba', which really pop out from the clipped foliage behind and prevent the space from looking too rigid.

At the time of writing we are in the process of redesigning the garden for new owners. The new brief is for a looser, softer, more luxuriant feel, so we will be using a richer, more tropical plant palette. The driveway will remain intact, but much of the rest of the space is being redesigned and replanted, so the garden beds surrounding the house will look completely different. In some ways it is sad to be changing a garden that is still young, but one thing I am learning in life is that change is constant and inevitable, whether I like it or not! The new owners want something lusher and more exotic, and I'm really chuffed that they have approached us for help.

TOP Variegated agave in Turkish whitewashed pots contrast nicely with large bromeliads in modern charcoal planters.

BOTTOM A viburnum hedge softens the boundary wall and creates definition under the neighbour's bamboo.

A 'Spartan' juniper conifer planted in a bronze striated pot.

Common jade hedge at the front of all the plantings – it will need cutting back hard from time to time to keep it under control.

A pair of olive trees defines the entry to the porte-cochere.

Shrub germander provides a silver highlight between the common jade and Gymea lily. The idea is to keep it tightly clipped, to contrast with the more organic form of the jade in front. The garden is still young in these images and will develop further over time.

At the top of the driveway we used hand-cut travertine, laid in a herringbone pattern – a lovely detail.

Sword-shaped leaves of Gymea lily contrast with the double-layered hedge in front.

Viburnum hedging.

The textured hedge of Chinese juniper is a bit more interesting than more traditional conifer hedges.

Agave specimens in whitewashed Turkish planters add character and architectural form, helping the garden look fresh and dynamic.

Boston ivy softens the lower half of the house. Giant mondo, great for shady spots, is planted underneath.

Clipped ball of shrub germander.

Persian shield is another great silver-foliaged plant.

Indian hawthorn.

Empress of Brazil bromeliad foliage provides lovely structural and colour contrast to the grey and green clipped forms in the layered scheme.

FORMAL GARDEN IDEAS

Formal, European-style gardens have been around since the sixteenth century, when gardens were designed around the sprawling palaces and official houses of the royalty and nobility. The French and the Italians were the masters of the craft, creating elaborate, over-the-top gardens where the lucky few could while away their time.

Since then, the formal style has been adapted and incorporated into modern culture the world over. Garden structure, layout and order are paramount for formal gardens, and the choice of plants and materials should be restrained and well-planned. Gardens are often laid out on an axis, with the viewpoint defining how the space is organised. Accents and focal points are created and counterbalanced. These points of reference are generally man-made, such as a large urn, seat or water feature, but could also include a particular tree or large plant within the landscape.

Even if your garden is not as large as those at Point Piper or Bellevue Hill (and very few are!) you can still replicate some of their features to create your own formal garden in a smaller space.

KEY POINTS

The first thing to note is that symmetry needs to be spot-on – if you want an urn in the courtyard, make sure it is placed right in the middle. If you are using a pair of feature plants, place them in exactly the same spot opposite each other. The geometry of the set-out is paramount. Frame doorways with a smart pair of planters or urns and mass-plant them with something soft, such as **cast-iron plant** (*Aspidistra elatior*) if it's shady, or **common jade** (*Crassula ovata*) if it's sunny. For something more contemporary, go for hard-edged cylinders and the thicker leaf of something like *Sansevieria* 'Congo'.

Add softening elements to create warmth and to prevent the garden from looking too rigid – at Point Piper we mass-planted the urns with **sedum** to spill over the tops. One way to create a focal point is to place one single beautiful object in the middle of a garden. It could be an antique Turkish urn, which need not even be planted – in a very small space, this would be enough on its own, just surrounded by a mass of **Japanese box** or a groundcover.

Exercise restraint with colour, ideally using only one flower colour; two max. The obvious classic choice is white, although you could try blues or purples to blend with this. Choose foliage colour over flowers and choose a variety of foliages – I am a big fan of bronzes, such as the rusty underside leaves of *Magnolia grandiflora* 'Little Gem' or *Kalanchoe* 'Copper Spoons', or bronze forms of **New Zealand flax** (*Phormium tenax*).

PLANTING STYLE

There are a few simple steps to follow to create formal gardens with a similar feel to these gardens in Point Piper and Bellevue Hill. The mantra is 'Keep it simple' – don't try to overdo it, or to fit too much in, as less is definitely more. This is especially true in smaller urban spaces.

It is really important to adhere to formal design principles to ensure a balanced and cohesive outcome. I like to create formal gardens which retain a natural aesthetic, and to introduce some softness to contrast with the formal lines of the structural landscape. It's about having some looseness in your foliage to contrast with the tightly clipped parts. A formal garden can look too cold and clinical if it's all clipped and manicured.

Planting schemes tend to be massed together. Hedges and screens of various sizes and scales are clipped and layered, but you can always add a more relaxed element to keep the space feeling warm and natural. For instance, in the main garden on the lawn area at Point Piper we introduced softer clumps of **euphorbia** and **bearded iris** (*Iris germanica*) to contrast with tightly clipped balls of **bush germander** (*Teucrium fruticans*).

Keep focal points bold and fresh – if you are using lots of hedging, avoid predictable, clipped topiary in planters, and try a sexier, looser feel, using **bromeliads** (such as *Alcantarea imperialis* 'Rubra') or a cycad such as **cardboard palm** (*Zamia furfuracea*), or succulents such as **aloe, agave** or **kalanchoe**. Architectural plants, such as **Gymea lily** (*Doryanthes excelsa*) or **Mauritius hemp** (*Furcraea foetida*), can make great focal points when contrasted with slick clipped hedges. In a small terrace garden you might find that one in the middle of a simple, square, low hedge of **Japanese box** (*Buxus microphylla* var. *japonica*) is enough by itself. What counts is the tension that blending the two forms will create, as one offsets the other. Use clipped or mounding specimens, mass-planted, to create the structure in the garden, then add the sexier forms to create interest.

TREES

Ornamental pears (*Pyrus calleryana*) are great deciduous trees to use in formal settings, with spring blossoms and autumn colour. There are many new varieties in different shapes and sizes, but check out '**Aristocrat**', the more upright and narrow '**Capital**' and the increasingly popular '**Chanticleer**'.

Chinese juniper (*Juniperus chinensis* 'Kaizuka') is a wonderfully rough-textured conifer with a pyramid shape, which can be clipped into an interesting hedge. **Spartan juniper** (*Juniperus chinensis* 'Spartan') is more of a full-bodied pencil pine, which responds well to clipping into a slick specimen. **Evergreen magnolia** (*Magnolia grandiflora*) is always a fine choice, with its vibrant green leaves, bronze undersides and dinner-plate-sized white flowers. 'Little Gem', 'Teddy Bear' or 'Greenback' are all good options.

MOUNDING AND CLIPPABLES

These are the essential plants that provide structure in a formal space and are often used en masse. **Japanese box** (*Buxus microphylla* var. *japonica*) is the most reliable, effective small hedge in warm climates and clips up so well. Let it grow bigger than you think it needs to be, as too small is too twee. If you live in a cold climate, plant the darker and pointy-leafed **English box** (*Buxus sempervirens*). **Common jade** (*Crassula ovarta*) is a strongly branched succulent which is an ideal choice for hedges where you want a softer, more organic feel, although it can grow quite large if left unchecked by regular pruning.

Try clipped balls of **shrub germander** (*Teucrium fruticans*) for a silver contrast. **Murraya** (*Murraya paniculata*) clips well into larger forms and is reliable in a semi-shaded position. *Pittosporum* 'Miss Muffet' is also a reliable performer and has a soft, mounding appearance. It is effective used in groups or lines to create amoebic forms, is great in sun or shade, and has a lovely, lime-green foliage darkening to a deep green over time. For something more unusual, try the succulent **elephant bush**, also commonly called **jade** (*Portulacaria afra*), which is very tough and drought-tolerant, and loves the sun.

ARCHITECTURALS

Architectural plants can draw the eye and create drama in any garden. A clump of **Gymea lily** (*Doryanthes excelsa*) or **Mauritius hemp** (*Furcraea foetida*) make a bold statement in formal spaces. Large bromeliads, such as *Alcantarea imperialis* 'Rubra', also create a strong accent when contrasted with slick hedges and solid forms. You could also try the **Mexican lily** (*Beschorneria yuccoides*), which has a strong foliage shape like the **yucca**, as well as a dramatic flower spike, or **cardboard palm** (*Zamia furfuracea*), a relative of the more common **cycad** (*Cycas revoluta*). It is a tough plant, with rounded leaves coming from arching stems, which are stiff like cardboard (hence the name).

GROUNDCOVERS AND FILLERS

You can fill in the spaces between clipped and architectural plants with interesting plants, which are looser, and smaller, and provide a third layer. Here are just some of the 'filler' plants available for you to choose from.

Convolvulus sabatius 'Two Moons' is a good choice if you need a mounding groundcover. Its (prolific) flowers are mainly white, with the odd blue one thrown in for good measure. The **New Zealand rock lily** (*Arthropodium cirratum*) has strappy, soft, grey-green leaves and white flowers in spring, and is great in the shade. **Bearded iris** (*Iris germanica*) has terrific foliage, with the added bonus of lovely purple or white flowers in summer. *Euphorbia* 'Black Bird', with its dark foliage, provides an interesting and unusual contrast within the smaller plants.

I love to use **giant mondo** (*Ophiopogon jaburan*) in shadier situations, as it is tough and clumping, with subtle white flower spikes in summer, and is also tolerant of dry conditions. **Cotyledon** (*Cotyledon orbiculata* 'Macrantha') is a succulent which performs terrifically massed in pots or under-planted in sunny spots. *Liriope* 'Evergreen Giant' is a grass-like plant which keeps its looks all year round. It is popular for a reason, performing well in both full sun and shade, with purple flower spikes at the end of summer. Finally, **plectranthus** is a great mid-level perennial with many different varieties. Try the silver-foliaged *Plectranthus argentatus* in sunnier spots, and the darker green and purple-leafed *Plectranthus ciliatus* in shadier areas.

VERTICALS

Don't overlook the vertical spaces in your formal garden. Covering walls, fences and other structures with climbers adds character, depth and age.

Choose your climber according to the sort of cover you want. If you are after a tight, evergreen cover, use **creeping fig** (*Ficus pumila*). For a soft, atmospheric character on a pergola, use deciduous **Boston ivy** (*Parthenocissus tricuspidata*), and consider as well its smaller-leafed brother, *Parthenocissus tricuspidata* 'Lowii', as well. For a scented mass of white, summer flowers use **star jasmine** (*Trachelospermum jasminoides*). It's a twiner, so you will need to provide supports for it to grow on, whereas the first two are self-supporting. All of these climbers are reliable performers, but they will need clipping to make sure they grow only where you want them to.

CREATE REPETITION

Repetition is about making a bold statement, and it is essential to all good design. The human eye likes to see the pattern of repeated objects; it creates strength and structure within a landscape.

That's why mass-planting will always be more effective than a mixture of plants with no connection to each other. If it works, do it again and then again if necessary. That doesn't mean that it all has to look the same, as contrast between foliage types is vital, but I think one of the worst things to see in a garden is a bit of this and a bit of that – it's dreadful!

You may choose to repeat the same pot; a series of three or five will make a bolder statement, and create a sense of continuity, consistency and connection. It can also create a sense of balance, and give structure to a more freeform arrangement elsewhere in the same space.

Here at Philip's nursery (see pages 182–183) the repeated plantings create massive visual impact. You could do something similar in a small space.

Here we used a series of the same white retro planters, planted with various different specimens.

There are lots of ways you can incorporate repetition into small spaces – it might be as simple as a custom rectangular planter with three striking *Agave ocahui* specimens surrounded by a mass of common jade.

At the townhouse in Walsh Bay, the repetition of this sandstone paving helps tie the space together by creating a strong, simple pattern. The orientation of the stone also stretches out the narrow space, appearing to give it more width (see pages 108–111).

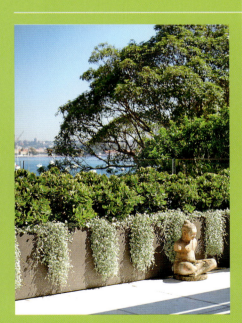

On the balcony at Darling Point the repetition of common jade with *Dichondra* 'Silver Falls' in the trough adds structure and looks chic (see pages 120–123).

At the Australian Film, Television and Radio School, using a series of oversized planters filled with exactly the same plants created structure on the rooftop (see pages 76–83).

A Relaxed Garden

BYRON BAY

—

Ever since I have lived in Australia, I have loved visiting the north coast of New South Wales about ten hours' drive from Sydney. I have made the trip up the Pacific Highway more times than I can remember, in the early days in my 1974 Volkswagen type 3 station wagon, which was prone to breaking down pretty frequently. These days I travel in greater comfort, and just last Christmas I enjoyed a very special bonding road trip with my fourteen-year-old godson, Hugo.

For the past six years I have been tinkering in a garden on the top of St Helena, just behind Byron Bay. It is possibly one of the most beautiful places on the planet. There is something of the divine about the landscape overlooking the Pacific Ocean at the most easterly point in Australia. The property, Byron View Farm, is the home of good friends. It is an old dairy farm of about 120 acres, sitting on a hillock with 360-degree views of the verdant, rolling hinterland, and views back to Lismore and up to the majestic Mount Warning on the Queensland border. There is always loads of weather up there; either the sun is beating down, it is blowing a gale, or it is pouring with rain.

I first met the owners in Sydney, when we started doing some garden work for them. When they first approached me about helping with the garden at Byron View Farm I was a little hesitant. My work in Sydney was really starting to take off and I was stretching myself to the limit, workwise. The last thing I needed was a big project out of town, and, knowing them, I knew they would have high expectations. So, I said 'no'.

Later that year, I was staying up around Byron and paid them a visit. I instantly changed my tune, falling in love with the place, hook, line and sinker. There is some amazing energy in the landscape up there, and something about the farm just grabbed hold of me. I couldn't help myself – I just started pruning the gardens surrounding the house, quickly realising that this was a project I would LOVE to be involved in.

We decided to work on the garden around the farmhouse in stages, and I have found myself making the trip up north every few months. As soon as I arrive, I am itching to get out and play in the garden; to clip back, transplant, prune and weed. There have been two stages to the garden's development – the first when the clients moved in, and the second about five years later, when they decided to build a guest cottage.

I love the ever-inquisitive cows that wander in the paddock beside the garden.

THE MAIN GARDEN

The brief for the garden surrounding the original Queenslander was pretty loose. Because we had worked together before, the clients trusted me to decide how the garden would look, although they did emphasise that they wanted the new garden to have almost zero maintenance. (This request is always a tough call, as no garden is maintenance-free, and at this point I normally have to manage the client's expectations as to what they will need to do, for the garden to develop.) We discussed a lush, relaxed, subtropical feel, and settled on a scheme using plants we knew would work up there.

The original weatherboard farmhouse and garden were quite neglected. Whilst the house potentially had killer views, many were obstructed, so one of our first tasks was to fix that. We cleared many of the trees and shrubs surrounding the farmhouse, opening up the views and creating some immediate space around the house. We also removed the lower limbs of many of the old pine trees which had originally been planted as a windbreak on the south side of the house, opening up views to the southwest.

Once we had cleared the old plants and unwanted foliage, we uncovered the original rock-edged, garden beds which surrounded the farmhouse. These were basically intact, so we decided to leave them there. Mindful of the 'low maintenance' brief, I opted for a mass of groundcover GARDENIA (*Gardenia augusta* 'Radicans') to fill most of these beds. These would grow to form a weed-repelling carpet of flowering, richly fragrant flowers. We added gingers and ornamental cardamom for height and foliage texture, and a few FRANGIPANI (*Plumeria rubra* var. *acutifolia*), as they fitted the soft subtropical feel perfectly, and were tough as well. At the back of the house we under-planted existing stands of BANGALOW PALM (*Archontophoenix cunninghamiana*) and GIANT BIRD OF PARADISE (*Strelitzia nicolai*) with BIRD'S NEST FERN (*Asplenium australasicum*), *Philodendron* 'Xanadu' and the ever-popular CENTURY PLANT (*Agave attenuata*).

The owners have a long-term vision for the property, and they planted some great new trees, including a majestic MORETON BAY FIG (*Ficus macrophylla*) and a pair of clumping and massive SWEET BAMBOO (*Dendrocalamus asper* 'Hitam') specimens that stand in a stately manner at the farm entrance, and will mature for future generations to enjoy.

THE GUEST COTTAGE GARDEN

A few years ago, the owners decided to build a cottage in the paddock next to the farmhouse to accommodate extra guests or rent out, and they asked us to come up with a design for the new garden. They wanted the cottage to mirror the simple design of the old farmhouse, with a wrap-around covered verandah to link the inside and outside.

They were concerned to maintain a sense of privacy in both the farmhouse and the guest cottage, and to maintain a sense of separation between them. I'm a massive fan of Yorkshire landscape sculptor Andy Goldsworthy; his dry stone walls are just sublime. As I started to think about the best way to create definition, it struck me that a dry stone wall would be the perfect solution. One of my favourite parts of the garden is a massive clump of giant bamboo sitting between the farmhouse and the cottage. Its mammoth stems groan in the wind like an old wooden boat on the high seas. In summer the heads of new growth resemble asparagus tips on growth hormones, rising out of the soil at least 20 centimetres each day. I decided

PREVIOUS PAGE The guest cottage. The 'Andy' dry stone wall defines the space between it and the original farmhouse. One of my favourite parts of this garden is the huge clump of bamboos on the left, which creak in the wind like an old wooden boat.

TOP Large right-angled steps of basalt crazy paving lead down to the L-shaped alfresco dining area in the guest cottage garden.

BOTTOM A lush, established layered garden surrounds the old farmhouse. Note the jungle-like foliage of giant bird of paradise on the left and the overhanging frangipani.

to encircle the base of the bamboo clump with a bold, earthy, dry stone wall, which would weave its way through the mature pine trees before seeming to disappear into the grass.

A local stonemason, Andy Walker, built the wall for us, and I love the fact that he used stones hand-selected from the surrounding fields. Because there are so many snakes in the area, the spaces between the stones are filled with concrete, as dry-packed walls make the perfect habitat for them. Inspired by Andy Goldsworthy and built by Andy Walker, it is now known as the 'Andy wall'. I love it and it's become one of the owners' favourite parts of the garden.

When we first saw the completed cottage it was just a square box in the middle of a field, and looked very uncomfortable. The brief for the cottage garden was to create a low-maintenance, soft garden, with areas for dining and relaxing alfresco, leaving room for a swimming pool in the future. We set about thinking how to bed this house in and make it feel at home, so to speak.

We developed a relaxed, simple scheme, with generous, softly curving garden beds surrounding the cottage, and a decomposed granite driveway and turning circle. We built pathways between the driveway and cottage in the same basalt that we used for the 'Andy wall', all laid in an informal 'crazy pave' pattern (irregular pieces all fitted together, with mortar between the stones). We then designed a set of large, right-angled steps leading down to an L-shaped built-in seat and a generous outdoor dining area. We levelled the paddock to accommodate a future pool at the end of the entertaining area.

We kept the planting simple, similar in style to the planting around the main house, although we had good-sized beds here so we could create some effective layering. We put together a palette of old-fashioned, softer, flowering plants, contrasted with bolder, more architectural forms. We planted large clumps of **NEW ZEALAND FLAX** (*Phormium tenax*) to demarcate the steps up to the balcony; and created borders of *Gardenia augusta* 'Radicans' (they grow prolifically in warm coastal climates) and the bright, purple-flowering **MEXICAN BUSH SAGE** (*Salvia leucantha*), which provided perfume and colour.

Natives also work well up here, so we offset clipped balls of **COASTAL ROSEMARY** (*Westringia fruticosa*) against the sword-shaped leaves of **SPEAR LILY** (*Doryanthes palmeri*), and introduced snaking bands of soft, grass-like *Lomandra longifolia* 'Tropic Belle' into the area between the two houses. This provided a green, sweeping version of the 'Andy wall', and linked the two together really well. We also planted an informal hedge of **INDIAN HAWTHORN** (*Rhaphiolepis indica*), moundings of the reliable *Pittosporum* 'Miss Muffet' and the purple-leaved **ARABIAN LILAC** (*Vitex trifolia* 'Purpurea').

The owners are very happy with the end result and how the garden is developing over time. She loves pottering about, pulling out odd weeds and cutting fresh flowers for the cottage for guests to enjoy, and he is addicted to his ride-on mower and keeping the grass tidy. He also loves the fact that he doesn't need to give the garden much attention, as it waits for me to visit and give things a good haircut, especially in winter when it needs a good, hard prune.

To this day I adore spending time at Byron View Farm. It's like a form of therapy every time I visit. I feel a stillness of spirit, as I completely relax and immerse myself in the surroundings. I start to wind down as soon as I arrive, forgetting about city life and its responsibilities. Usually I wake up with the sun, head outdoors with my cup of tea and just soak up the peace and quiet. An eerie mist hovers over the hollows below, the cows are starting to move in the lush paddocks surrounding the house, and the birds are making their first morning calls. It really does feel like heaven.

TOP The 'Andy' wall seems to just disappear into the grass.

BOTTOM The base of this clump of bamboos is defined perfectly by the 'Andy' wall.

Some visits I tend to garden more than others, but I will always tinker with something. Between visits I often think about how the plants are growing, and I'm always contemplating my next trip up north. One of my favourite jobs is to give the bamboo a 'Brazilian', by trimming out all of the lateral growth up to about two metres high, showing off the massive fat stems.

Some of my favourite things in the garden are the lichen on the old, wooden fences, the ever-inquisitive cows in the surrounding paddocks, the rickety old seat that is somehow still standing, the massive grass trees that just poke out of the lawn and the fresh, gold husks of the new big, fat, bamboo stems. I love the mix of nana and glamour! The combination of soil moisture, warm atmosphere and deep, rich volcanic soils creates ideal growing conditions, and the garden is quickly maturing and starting to own the space.

LEFT Lichen-encrusted tree trunks.

OPPOSITE Just the place to contemplate life first thing in the morning with a cup of tea as the mist rolls in.

Mexican bush sage provides a mass of flowering colour.

New Zealand flax is planted on either side of the steps, giving a sense of formality.

Architectural leaves of Gymea lily provide structure.

Mounding form of Pittosporum 'Miss Muffet'.

Good old agaves provide form against the basalt stonework.

Wide, wraparound basalt steps lead down to the future swimming pool and dining area.

A pair of old urns planted with begonias are a nod to the property's classic, old-fashioned feel.

Multi-branched Bangalow palms grow so well here in their native North Coast habitat.

Lomandra is a super-tough, versatile, native grass-like plant with great movement.

Clipped silver-foliaged coastal rosemary contrasts beautifully with the more random shape of lomandra, giving this garden an organic structure.

RELAXED GARDEN IDEAS

More and more people are coming to us these days wanting a soft aesthetic – 'green', 'lush' and 'oasis' are the words often used. I think this is a reaction to our residential urban spaces being too built-up.

When creating a more relaxed style of garden, you need a looser, more natural aesthetic. That said, I will often include some of the elements of a more formal garden to create a balance somewhere between the two. Even in a softer garden you still need order, cohesion, definition and elements of control, otherwise it can just end up looking like a rambling mess. So, for example, in the garden at Byron View Farm we defined the steps up to the guest cottage by planting **New Zealand flax** (*Phormium tenax*) symmetrically on either side, and placing a pair of white **frangipani** (*Plumeria rubra* var. *acutifolia*) strategically on each side of the verandah.

KEY POINTS

Organic lines and softer stonework are a perfect fit when you are choosing materials for the structural elements, like walls and paving. There's no need to be too rigid with materials or layout. Dry-packed stone walls and crazy paving sandstone (random pieces of sandstone laid together like a jigsaw, with mortared joints) work well, as do recycled bricks, with their instant-aged aesthetic. Try experimenting with different laying patterns, mixing things up a bit. Bricks work well with sandstone, and an aged brick wall with a soft climber can look sensational.

Even if your home is contemporary or minimalist in style, you might still want a softer-style garden. Here I suggest you use slick, more geometric elements such as bluestone, granite or concrete for the paving and walls, but choose a planting scheme which softens and contrasts with the structure to give the right balance.

PLANTING STYLE

Plant positioning in a garden like this is relaxed, and the layout is generally more asymmetrical. You might still use feature plants to frame entries and give definition, but other planting needs to be looser and more natural.

It's still important to choose a core group of plants, to ensure there is cohesion and structure within the garden – try to avoid creating a garden with one specimen of this and one specimen of that. Groups of three or five of the same plant in serpentine-like swathes or mass drifts will create an impact, whilst still retaining a natural feel.

One way to create a softer look is to layer your plants. Be sure to remember the basic rule – smaller specimens at the front, and taller ones towards the rear, so all the plants can be seen and can receive sunlight. Try combining plants of different heights, including trees, shrubs, architectural foliage, clumping plants, strappy leaf plants, low hedging, groundcovers and climbing plants.

You might also want to group together plants with different textured foliage groups, so that each will complement the other. Creating subtle contrasts between foliage forms is the key to visual success in any garden space. So, for example, you might use plants with naturally mounded forms such as *Pittosporum* 'Miss Muffet' next to the grassy-like leaves of **giant mondo grass** (*Ophiopogon jaburan*), and the architectural form of **century plant** (*Agave attenuata*).

When using a number of different species in an informal bed, tie them all together by using one plant at the front. Groundcover **gardenia** (*Gardenia augusta* 'Radicans') works well, or try **giant mondo grass** (*Ophiopogon jaburan*) if you prefer a ribbon-like leaf, or a low succulent such as **echeveria** if you have a sunny spot. Good trees to use include **crepe myrtle** (*Lagerstroemia indica*), **Japanese maple** (*Acer palmatum*), **ornamental pear** (*Pyrus calleryana*) or **Chinese tallow tree** (*Sapium sebiferum*). Depending on the size of your garden, you could use a single specimen, a pair to give structure to either side of a pathway or entrance, or several to create cohesion. Low hedges provide structure, and these can be clipped tight and square or left softer, rounder, and more relaxed.

If you want to use a climber, you could use two or more varieties, rather than just sticking to one. Try using **ornamental grape** (*Vitis vinifera*) as well as **Boston ivy** (*Parthenocissus tricuspidata*), or combine **star jasmine** (*Trachelospermum jasminoides*) with the smaller-leafed variety of **Boston ivy** (*Parthenocissus tricuspidata* 'Lowii'). Plant climbers and screens together, and let the tendrils of the climber snake through the patterns of the screen.

You will use more flowering plants in a less formal garden, but do exercise some restraint when selecting your colour scheme. Stick to purples, blues, whites and greens for a classic, cooler feel. You might add splashes of orange for something a little 'hotter' looking. Don't forget to consider foliage colour – silvers, light greens, dark greens and bronzes all complement each other. Avoid harsh, garish foliage colours such as yellows, purples and reds. I used white and purple against green foliage at Byron View Farm; it's a classic colour scheme that always works. Finally, make sure you choose a selection that will give you flowers throughout the year.

'INSTANT COUNTRY'

Begonias are so old-school and so cool. Cane begonias can reach 1.5 metres and have clusters of nana-like pink blooms. Smaller annual varieties provide great colour, and work well either in pots or grouped together in beds, although I suggest you stick to one colour. Salvias are classic country plants which flower profusely. The purple one I used at Byron View Farm, **Mexican bush sage** (*Salvia leucantha*), has the perfect soft aesthetic and never stops giving. Plus, it is more reliable and less twee than lavender. **Rosemary** (*Rosmarinus officinalis*) is also terrific and performs well in full sun.

TREES

Ivory curl tree (*Buckinghamia celsissima*) is a gorgeous small tree, covered in cream flowers mid-summer – it's really tough and a great performer. **Japanese maple** (*Acer palmatum*) is a wonderfully soft, deciduous tree available in many different varieties. Its delicate leaves make it ideal for a gentle aesthetic. Other varieties of maple I like to use include the stunning *Acer palmatum* 'Sango-kaku' (also sold as 'Senkaki'), which I love for its coral pink stems, *A. palmatum* 'Bloodgood', whose leaves are black and red in spring, turning to purple with pale green veins in summer, and *A. japonicum* 'Vitifolium' also known as the vine-leafed full moon maple.

Crepe myrtles (both *Lagerstroemia indica* and *L. fauriei*) are firm favourites of mine. These small trees offer good autumn colour and vibrant late-spring to summer flowers. Try the white flowering cultivars '**Natchez**' and '**Kiowa**', or, if you want a pink flower, select either '**Biloxi**' or '**Yuma**'.

MOUNDINGS AND CLIPPABLES

Indian hawthorn (*Rhaphiolepis indica*) is very useful in a softer planting scheme. 'Oriental Pearl' or 'Snow Maiden' are two terrific compact cultivars of **Indian hawthorn**, producing prolific, small white flowers in late winter and spring. Group them together to contrast with grasses or more architectural planting. *Rhaphiolepis indica* can reach 2 metres or more in height, and is great as an informal hedge or low screen, and many of the modern cultivars are more compact with the bonus of larger flowers. Many produce less fruit than the species, reducing their weed potential. Any of the species mentioned on pages 42–43 in the section on formal gardens, or on pages 72–73 in the section on coastal gardens, such as **westringia, pittosporum, liquorice plant** (*Helichrysum petiolare*), **Japanese box, murraya and bush germander** will work well. Try planting a group of three together, each one a different species, and let them grow to different sizes. **Murraya** (*Murraya paniculata*) is a good larger choice, with **bush germander** (*Teucrium fruticans*) and *Pittosporum* 'Miss Muffet' making up the medium and smaller size. Or choose the same species for all three then clip them more softly than you would in a formal setting so they are a little fluffier.

ARCHITECTURALS

You can choose foliage which is a little softer for less formal gardens, though you could also use any of the foliage mentioned in the section on formal gardens on pages 42–43.

New Zealand flax (*Phormium tenax*) has a soft, sword-leafed form, and you can get some lovely bronze-foliaged varieties. I like to use the bronze foliage variety, *Phormium tenax* 'Purpurea'. The huge flower spikes also look great dried. The **spider lily** (*Crinum pedunculatum*) has thick, fleshy green leaves which grow from a central bulb. The metre-high foliage is just as beautiful as the large, delicate white flowers that sit just above the leaves during spring and summer.

Agaves are perfect for adding structure on a smaller scale, and there are so many different species and varieties to choose from. If you want something a little different from the popular *Agave attenuata*, try *A. ocahui*, *A. victoriae-reginae* or *A. parryi*. Rosette-forming succulents, including **echeveria**, also create fascinating patterns with their foliage and look good massed together in contrast with plants with looser foliage.

GRASSES AND GRASS-LIKE PLANTS

A tough perennial that just keeps going is **wild iris** (*Dietes grandiflora*), which forms clumps of fine, sword-shaped leaves with masses of yellow, purple and white iris flowers – each open for just a day, but with many buds on each stem guaranteeing a long flowering period.

Miscanthus is a really useful ornamental grass, with a great form. *Miscanthus sinensis* 'Zebrinus' has striped horizontal markings on the leaves and will grow to 1.5 metres or more. *M. sinensis* 'Kleine Silberspinne' is more compact, with silver-green leaves and large plumes of red-brown flowers in autumn.

Coral or firecracker plant (*Russelia equisetiformis*) works well as a spill-over or groundcover, especially in warmer climates. The coral-red flowers can be a little showy, so you might choose the more classic, ivory-coloured 'Lemon Falls' for a more subdued flowering scheme.

Coastal Garden

WHALE BEACH

—

I often think that there are a lot of similarities between relationships with people and relationships with gardens. Great gardens take time to develop – nothing good generally comes from a twenty-four-hour encounter (I'd like to see some of those 'makeover' show gardens after two years). If you neglect your garden, this generally leads to disaster, but too much attention or smothering can have the same effect. Gentle nurturing and sincere effort over a period of time usually produce the best results, and then the rewards can be huge.

We first started looking at this coastal garden about six years ago, when the clients were rebuilding, transforming the house from a humble beach house into a swanky coastal pad. Their aim was to create a weekend retreat, an oasis where they could come to relax and escape their busy schedules. My relationship with the garden has grown and endured over the years, although unfortunately I don't manage to get there nearly as much as I would like to. Usually Nick and I will visit a couple of times a year to see if anything needs to be freshened up.

When I first visited the property, it was quite an adventure scrambling around the overgrown, terraced gardens leading down to the ocean cliffs. Although the gardens were a bit wild, I could see that at some stage they had been tended by a garden enthusiast. There were remnants of mature, stone fruit specimens such as peach, almond and mango trees, as well as banana trees, daffodils and even a few roses. Knowing that the garden had previously been loved made me want to return it to its former glory. I loved the sense of rambling in this overgrown 'wilderness', and I wanted to preserve some of the magic of the space.

Most of the garden is at the rear of the house – full-length balconies stretch the width of the property, and the pool shimmers below, before the garden falls away steeply to the ocean. On the pool level we created a slick resort feel, installing elements like warm walnut travertine next to the blackbutt decking. The owners are keen entertainers, and wanted lots of seating and lounges around the pool, so we created big, wide, built-in day beds and added some round Dedon furniture. We placed three of our Geo screens on the boundary wall, creating a strong focal point and also providing privacy. Around the pool we used a series of large, wood-fired planters with cycads and succulents to green up and soften the corners and edges.

Lower down, we kept the sandstone terracing largely intact, as I wanted to retain some of the garden's informality. We rebuilt the stone walls, and improved access by creating a second set of sandstone stairs at the far side of the terraces. For the floor

One of the heavily planted gravelled terraces leading down to the ocean. On the right, starting at the front, you can see agave, leafless bird of paradise, clipped Indian hawthorn, and bushy euphorbia. An existing giant bird of paradise frames the image.

surface we used a combination of crazy paving steps and soft brown gravel paths. The crunchy stones underfoot add great texture, and I love the sound and feel as you walk through; it's so relaxing and evocative. Hearing the ocean crashing on the cliffs below and the soft crunch of gravel underfoot certainly takes your mind off the city.

The plants had to be tough and able to thrive in the exposed site. We developed a lush, coastal palette, with a loose Mediterranean influence, blending strong, architectural foliage with softer, mounding clipped forms including succulents, native grasses and ferns in more sheltered spots. The overall scheme is very plant-driven, as I didn't want to create a heavily 'designed' or contrived space; it had to be relaxed, loose and enticing. We created a timber pad at the base of the garden, overlooking the ocean, as our client wanted a place just in front of the cliffs, where he could work, or just sit and contemplate life, the universe and everything in between.

We had to be ruthless with most of the original plants, which were generally in poor health and didn't work with the new planting scheme, but we did manage to save many of the smaller perennials, which we moved to more suitable positions. The garden now has a great sense of exploration and discovery. Walking down through the terraced gardens to the sea is a journey in itself, and it's a joy to just meander and lose yourself in it all, as each twist reveals another aspect of the ocean below.

LEFT We transplanted some existing agapanthus, which is such a hardy plant.

TOP RIGHT Our Geo screens define the rear boundary, with advanced cycads in wood-fired pots in front, and some sun-loving agaves on the left.

BOTTOM RIGHT The king of architectural plants, the prehistoric-looking felt plant, with its amazing texture and dramatic form.

Rush-leaf bird of paradise is a tough flowering species ideal for coastal locations.

Soft gravel paths feel wonderfully crunchy underfoot. They border these informal sandstone terraced walls.

Giant bird of paradise foliage works well here, giving a tropical feel.

Leaves of red-edge screw pine (a species of pandanus) dominate the terrace.

Mounding form of Indian hawthorn.

Echeverias grow easily in amongst the rocks and are ideal for coastal locations.

Architectural form of dragon tree stands out above the lower clipped foliage.

Bronze cabbage palm foliage contrasts well with the grey and greens elsewhere in the garden.

Coastal rosemary, a tough native, is just perfect for this exposed position.

There were good old agapanthus throughout the existing garden – we moved them to where they were more effective.

COASTAL GARDEN IDEAS

A coastal garden is similar in feel to a relaxed garden, and you can follow the same basic design guidelines, although it can be even looser, with a slightly wilder aesthetic – nature in the raw, a little more untamed. Natural tones and textures such as greys, greens, bronzes and browns all combine well to give that feeling of the sun-bleached tones of the coast.

KEY POINTS

Nowhere is plant selection more crucial than in the coastal garden. Plants here have to cope with a lot: exposure to the elements, high winds laden with salt air, sandy soils with poor moisture retention and often full sun for most of the day. Choose your plants with care – it's a good idea to look at what is growing well in similar positions in nearby gardens. Smaller plants will cope better with rough conditions and are less susceptible to wind burn or physical harm.

For the harder surfaces in a coastal garden, it's all about keeping things natural. Gravel paths are easy to install and feel fantastic underfoot. They literally slow you down and force you to relax! Timber is also a great choice. Allow decks to grey and weather naturally. As a general rule, timbers that start off red (for example, red gum), will eventually turn silver. Don't forget sandstone, which gives a soft, organic coastal look. Crazy paving always works well. Use a rectilinear style if you want a more formal, tighter feel.

Stone retaining walls are soft and earthy with great texture and look great with some sedum plants or suchlike spilling over. Keep the style fairly loose and informal. Aim for a random dry-stone-wall feel, rather than using rigid, regular pieces all mortared together. Timber walls also work well as a cheaper option – try using treated pine sleepers. You could stain them black or charcoal for a crisp, striking look. Or use wide decking timber, laid horizontally, to clad a masonry wall.

PLANTING STYLE

Consider using plants which occur naturally on the coast, as they are likely to be more tolerant of prevailing conditions. This is especially true of trees and larger specimens, given their heightened exposure.

As a general rule, group plants together in threes and fives for impact, choosing plants with contrasting foliage to offset each other. Plants with silver foliage are usually tougher, and will withstand the salt air better, than large-leafed green foliage.

Plant either clippable or mounding specimens to add the element of control and definition which you need in all gardens. The coastal garden should have a natural, slightly wild aesthetic, so don't make it too rigid. Softer clipping and more informal shapes will look more natural than tightly clipped balls.

TREES

All **banksias,** including *Banksia integrifolia*, *B. serrata* and *B. robur*, work beautifully in coastal locations with their wild and natural habit, and different forms. **Coastal hibiscus** (*Hibiscus tiliaceus*) looks a bit softer, with larger round leaves and flowers that change colour from yellow to orange to red in the course of their one-day life. **Tuckeroo** (*Cupaniopsis anacardioides*) is a tough, adaptable small tree with dark green, leathery leaves and yellow flowers which is great for screening in exposed areas.

MOUNDINGS AND CLIPPABLES

Coastal rosemary (*Westringia fruticosa*) is a nice choice for exposed areas as it is tough, and responds well to pruning. **Liquorice plant** (*Helichrysum petiolare*) has soft, grey-green foliage and a very coastal look. The cultivar 'Limelight' has a fresh, light-green foliage and is very hardy with a little shelter, although it is not as salt-tolerant as **coastal rosemary**. *Pittosporum* 'Miss Muffet' is tough and versatile, with a naturally mounding habit, although it can be clipped to keep it down in size. It produces scented white flowers in summer. **Blue jade** (*Crassula* 'Blue Bird') is a plant with grey-blue foliage and is tough, reliable and a naturally mounding performer. The regular, glossy, green-leafed **common jade** (*Crassula ovata*) is also perfect for areas exposed to salt, and clips up well.

ARCHITECTURALS

Mauritius hemp (*Furcraea foetida*) is a very striking succulent that is bombproof, and its dark green, sword-shaped leaves can grow up to 2 metres high. Variegated specimens are generally smaller, and they make great accent plants. Plant in clumps and give them room to grow.

Firesticks (*Euphorbia tirucalli*) is an unusual looking plant which is perfect for coastal locations, because the shrub has no leaves from which water can evaporate, and the vibrant green stems have modified to photosynthesise. It can be pruned if it becomes too large (though watch the milky sap, as it can irritate the skin).

Dragon tree (*Dracaena draco*) is another toughie with great form, which is ideally suited to coastal gardens. It prefers full sun. **Felt plant** (*Kalanchoe beharensis*) is one of my favourite plants. With its felt-like leaves, almost 40 centimetres across, it has wonderful sculptural value. It loves full sun and well-drained soil. The cultivar 'Oakleaf' has smaller leaves and is a more compact variety, growing to about 1 metre high. *Kalanchoe orgyalis* 'Copper Spoons' has a wonderful texture and a lovely oval leaf, which is bronze on the top side and silver underneath.

GRASSES AND GRASS-LIKE PLANTS

Pennisetum, poa and the grass-like **lomandra** (*Lomandra longifolia*) are all tough and work well in a coastal garden. They have movement and softness, and set off the mounding, clipped and architecturals perfectly.

GROUNDCOVERS

Loads of groundcovers and succulents are perfect for coastal plantings. You could try **blue chalksticks** (*Senecio serpens*) and I also love the soft, pink, daisy-like flowers of the **giant pigface** (*Carpobrotus acinaciformis*) and the vibrant pinks, white, mauves and orange flowers of **ice plant** (*Lampranthus aurantiacus*). **Gazania** (*Gazania rigens*) has lovely silvery foliage and gaudy flowers in oranges and yellows – seek out sterile hybrid cultivars if you are concerned about their reputation for weediness.

A couple of interesting groundcover cultivars of larger native trees are worth a look. *Banksia integrifolia* 'Roller Coaster' is a great native spillover and groundcover in a coastal spot, as is *Casuarina glauca* 'Cousin-It' with its needle-like leaves and low, weeping growth.

CREATE TEXTURE

It's important to think about how you can use contrasting textures to enhance your garden by creating tension and thus adding interest to the landscape. You might place a plant with a large, open foliage next to one with a small, clumping one, or you might put a slick, white, contemporary planter next to an old terracotta or brass urn. Try using a weathered, rough-textured piece of stone as a backdrop to a striking succulent or planting a spiky agave next to a soft, fleshy jade tree – contrasting a spiky foliage plant with something softer helps one to stand out from the other. You can also introduce a contrast in textures to your ornamentation – an old, metal screen might look great on a slick, rendered wall, for instance.

A Garden of Pots and Planters

AUSTRALIAN FILM, TELEVISION AND RADIO SCHOOL

―

This project came about because Sandra Levy, CEO of the Australian Film, Television and Radio School (AFTRS), saw one of our massive bullet planters in the Garden Life shop window on her daily drive to work along Cleveland Street in Sydney.

The AFTRS rooftop was a huge, tiled outdoor area facing north-west, extremely exposed, and blasted by sunshine all day. A stark awning provided the only shade. It was the most uninviting space imaginable, without a single plant. Our brief was to create a serious rooftop garden; a green retreat for staff to work in, or just somewhere to enjoy tranquil, reflective moments.

We wanted to create a series of separate garden areas, without actually making individual 'rooms'. To do this you need to use serious scale – it's about putting in place oversized planters and advanced plant material, then layering that down to a more human level with different textures and foliage, creating interest on different levels.

The challenge when relying solely on pots and planters to make a garden is to ensure that the end result doesn't look like you have used exactly that. You need to give a lot of thought to the colour, texture and ratios of the containers – the trick is to create clever compositions of contrasting forms, which, combined, create the feeling of a cohesive garden space.

We developed a low-maintenance plant palette that would thrive in the exposed, sunny aspect. Although it was a commercial office space, we wanted the garden to have a slick residential feel, a private and intimate funky vibe. The design centred on a series of six of the massive bullet planters that Sandra had originally seen in the shop window. We planted them with super-advanced specimens of **WEEPING LILLYPILLY** (*Waterhousea floribunda*) (anything smaller would have simply disappeared into the space), then arranged the planters to provide some intimate breakout spaces within the area.

Next, we grouped together collections of rectangular and square planters of varying sizes, and massed them with contrasting foliage under the awning. We mixed the sword-like leaves of **BLACK NEW ZEALAND FLAX** (*Phormium tenax* 'Platts Black') with **DWARF JAPANESE PITTOSPORUM** (*Pittosporum tobira* 'Wheelers Dwarf'), and placed *Kalanchoe orgyalis* 'Copper Spoons' next to the **RUSH-LEAVED BIRD OF PARADISE** (*Strelitzia juncea*). These are all great plants for exposed rooftop gardens as they are bombproof – they thrive in hot sun, cope with high winds and are resilient

We anchored this space with oversized bullet pots, planted with weeping lillypilly and under-planted with cardboard palm and white-flowering ice plant. Tree aloe in large cubed pots provide a strong contrast.

in dry conditions (especially **KALANCHOE** and **STRELITZIA**). The vigorous deciduous climber **BOSTON IVY** (*Parthenocissus tricuspidata*) is now starting to grow up over the awning, softening it and giving it character.

We also created an area of succulents in one corner of the garden. Succulents are great because they are so drought-hardy, and low-maintenance. By mass planting with contrasting foliage, we created patterns and interest within each planter. We fitted industrial castors to the modular planters, enabling them to be moved easily if the layout needed to be changed for events.

There is now a sense of discovery in the garden; it's full of interest, and provides a welcome respite from office life. When we returned to shoot the images for this book I was delighted to see staff enjoying it – having lunch and working around the tables. It was exactly how we wanted the space to be used. What a transformation a few big, beautiful plants and a well-designed garden can make to our urban workspaces! I am sure that having contented and refreshed staff makes the work environment happier and healthier. It's a shame that more businesses don't recognise this and invest in creating beautiful outdoor spaces for their staff. Let's have more lush rooftops on our commercial buildings!

A further step would be to create a food-producing space, and get staff involved in growing herbs and vegies they can use. The conditions are perfect up there, and there's plenty of sun, which is really the main ingredient. Growing food in pots is very simple, it's all about starting with a good-quality potting mixture and adding lots of organic nutrients such as worm wee, manures and liquid feeds (for more on this, a favourite topic of mine, see chapter 3). Of course, more maintenance is needed when you are growing food, but it is rewarding, relaxing work, and would help make being at work more enjoyable.

ABOVE Before – the rooftop was the most uninviting space imaginable, with not a single plant.

TOP RIGHT Transformation. In the front left corner you can see the bombproof rush-leaf bird of paradise, and behind it Gymea lilies. Boston ivy is starting to creep up and soften the awning.

BOTTOM RIGHT We placed succulents on the tables to add some interest – they are such hardy plants.

This furry-leafed form of kalanchoe is a favourite of mine. It loves the sun and will grow taller than the cotyledons, providing a perfect silvery-grey backdrop.

Cotyledons, with their big, verdant, fleshy leaves form the middle band of planting here.

Lightweight planters in different heights and sizes create interest.

Silver-green echeverias planted at the front. These guys need full sun.

Create interest in a large pot by banding together two or three plants with subtly contrasting foliage.

A bronze form of echeveria – they come in all colours and shapes.

Rush-leaf bird of paradise used again in this space, as it's such a reliable performer in containers, especially in a really exposed space like this one.

We applied Murobond Bridge Paint to these galvanised cylinders to add an industrial texture.

Weeping lillypilly.

Textured leaves of cardboard palms and the trailing white flowering ice plant add interest underneath the weeping lillypilly.

We used a series of six of our massive bullet bowls, 150 centimetres in diameter, to give the space structure and order.

POTS AND PLANTERS IDEAS

Sometimes the only way to grow plants in an outdoor space is to use pots. You may live in a high-rise apartment with a balcony, or be lucky enough to have an extensive roof terrace. Your backyard might be paved and you might want to create an instant garden on a budget. You can see the transformation of the AFTRS roof terrace from a brutally exposed, tiled shocker into a welcoming retreat just by using planters. Although the AFTRS garden is one large rooftop, all we did was to create a series of connecting smaller spaces within it. Let's look at how you can create a scheme just using just pots and planters.

KEY POINTS

There is a good rule of thumb when selecting from the vast array of pots and plants on the market. I call it the '70/20/10 rule'. Keep the majority of pots and plants (say 70 per cent) very simple. These will provide the structure and cohesion for the basic layout. Buy good quality planters, without going overboard. At AFTRS we used mostly off-white planters in understated rectangles and round shapes. The plants were a mixture of mostly soft-foliaged plants – nothing too showy, but creating the ambience and providing good bulk and scale.

Next, introduce a different style of planter by way of contrast. The finish could be different, and preferably the shape as well. Aim for these to make up about 20 per cent of your pots. At AFTRS we used hand-painted galvanised steel cylinders. Introducing pots with a different shape, texture and colour created interest. We planted these with some sexier foliaged plants including **rush-leaved bird of paradise** (*Strelitzia juncea*), *Kalanchoe orgyalis* 'Copper Spoons' and **black New Zealand flax** (*Phormium tenax* 'Platts Black').

The final 10 per cent of pots and plants can be more out-there. Try a couple of mad architectural plants, or a beautiful, antique, brass planter – a hero piece, like an old Turkish stone mortar planted full of succulents. At AFTRS we used an advanced **tree aloe** (*Aloe barberae*) and also a large specimen of **firesticks** (*Euphorbia tirucalli*) for the 'look at me' plants.

In a small residential setting you might have five fairly generic specimens to provide the structure (or screening, or whatever is needed), two pots with a more textured finish and a different plant style, and then one piece that stands out and has a bit of the 'wow' factor.

PLANTING STYLE

First things first – what do you want to achieve? Privacy and a feeling of intimacy? A general softening and greening? Or do you want to add drama and a strong architectural look? Are you aiming for a formal or informal space? You can really create any style of garden using pots and planters – formal and French-inspired, or relaxed and contemporary; a lot comes down to the plants you choose.

For a more formal garden, as always, you need symmetry and balance, with clipped hedges and mounded forms mixed with looser specimens for contrast. Dense foliage with small leaves, such as *Pittosporum* 'Miss Muffet', **common jade** (*Crassula ovata*) and hedges of **Japanese box** (*Buxus microphylla*) are generally more formal (depending on the layout of the garden).

For something less formal, use large plants to create structure, then add clusters of smaller plants. A series of five big **aloes** in simple, large planters will give an ultra-contemporary and architectural look, then you could use small-leafed hedging or mounding plants to make up most of the garden's structure.

It's important to minimise exposed areas of hard surfaces; the floor, the walls and even the pots themselves. One good solution is to under-plant taller plants in pots with groundcovers that will trail down over the edges of the pots to soften the look. In larger pots plant several specimens to give a fuller, more layered feel.

OPPOSITE Trio of dragon trees in crisp, white cylinders.

COMMON JADE
(CRASSULA OVATA)

I can't remember when I started using **jade**, but it is the one plant I keep coming back to. It works in full sun and also full shade, on ocean fronts, or in a sheltered garden. Don't overwater it, as it loves being dry – perfect if you go away for a few weeks. Prune it to shape – it makes a fab informal hedge in a slick trough or a big clipped sphere. It produces small, white, star-shaped flowers in winter.

BRAZILIAN WALKING IRIS
(NEOMARCIA GRACILIS)

This plant gets its name from its spreading nature. After the beautiful, blue flowers have died down, new plants emerge, which you can cut off to use elsewhere in the garden. Left to their own devices, the stems bend down so the new plants at the tips can take root in the ground allowing the plant to spread as if it is 'walking'. These babies grow readily and can be cut off to plant elsewhere in the garden. These are best in the shade or morning sun – keep them out of the afternoon sun. They are good in hanging pots, vertical gardens or shady corners, or as soft foliage under-planting larger plants.

THE AGAVE FAMILY
(AGAVACEAE)

Agave have been popular now for the last ten to fifteen years. *Agave attenuata* has been a little overused, though with good reason, as it is another great performer with a beautiful leaf arrangement. For something just as effective, but a little different, try *Agave ocahui* or *Agave americana* 'Mediopicta'. Use them sparingly, in feature pots, as a contrast to hedging or small-leafed plants. Agave are best in all-day or at least half-day sun, and you should water them monthly. Remove the baby plants and grow them in small pots.

RUSH-LEAFED BIRD OF PARADISE
(STRELITZIA JUNCEA)

This is a striking and architectural plant that can add some drama and minimalist form to a contemporary garden. The common **bird of paradise** (*Strelitzia reginae*) is also worth a mention, as it's very tough and adaptable. It works in either full sun or part shade, though it flowers less in the shade. It tolerates dry spells and general neglect, you just need to trim off old flowers and leaves. Use it in feature pots to contrast with smaller-leafed plants.

GIANT MONDO GRASS
(OPHIOPOGON JABURAN)

This is a great filler plant, good for borders, under-planting or mass planting in pots. As its common name suggests, it's a big version of the more common **mondo grass** (*Ophiopogon japonicus*), growing up to 60 centimetres high and 40 centimetres wide, but just as tough and adaptable as good old mondo grass. It is best in shade or morning sun, and is tolerant of dry spells once established. I like to use it in slim troughs in shady spots, or just massed in one pot.

FIDDLE-LEAF FIG
(FICUS LYRATA)

I love the big-veined leaf of this medium-sized tree, which is thought to be the fig-leaf used by Adam and Eve in Biblical times to cover their bits! It's best in the shade or the morning sun, and makes a tall, striking indoor plant, but do keep it moist. It is also great in a large pot under-planted with smaller-leafed plants to add some texture – you can always prune or repot it if it gets too big.

DICHONDRA ARGENTEA 'SILVER FALLS'

This is a silvery-grey trailing plant which, unlike the closely related **kidney-weed** (*Dichondra repens*), does not become highly invasive. **'Silver Falls'** is best in a sunny spot, but it also does well in part sun, part shade. It is tolerant of dry spells, but does better if kept damp. It is perfect for trailing down walls or softening the sides of pots and troughs.

MISTLETOE CACTUS (RHIPSALIS BACCIFERA)

I never tire of using this trailing, green spaghetti-like plant; it just has the best texture. It grows well outdoors in part to full sun and is very adaptable. It can be kept very dry and tolerates some neglect, but soak it when you do water it, then allow the water to drain. Use it in hanging pots or for trailing down walls and the sides of pots.

CHINESE JUNIPER (JUNIPERUS CHINENSIS 'KAIZUKA' ALSO SOLD AS 'KETELEERI')

This is a great textured conifer, superb for privacy screening and creating dividers. It needs sun for at least half the day. You can prune it to shape it as required. Plant in big troughs to give it room to grow.

CARDBOARD PALM (ZAMIA FURFURACEA)

This is a slow-growing relative of the more common **cycad** (*Cycas revoluta*). I love its pre-historic, ancient feel. It likes full or part sun and is pretty tough, so it can tolerate dry spells. It works well in feature pots – plant *Dichondra* 'Silver Falls' around the base to flow down the sides.

WEEPING LILLYPILLY (WATERHOUSEA FLORIBUNDA)

These are the big trees we used at the Australian Film, Television and Radio School as they are great when you want some real scale. They are native to New South Wales. You will need a big planter, at least 120 centimetres in diameter. They need at least half a day of sunshine, and to be kept well-watered and mulched so they don't dry out. They work well as dividers or screens when you want a softer look.

FIRESTICKS OR PENCIL TREE (EUPHORBIA TIRUCALLI)

These are highly unusual succulents with an interesting texture formed by the smooth, green, cylindrical leafless branches. They can grow into small trees 4.5 to 9 metres tall if you let them, but are mostly maintained as shrubs. They need at least half a day of sunshine. They are pretty tough so you can let them dry out for long spells, then water them well. Don't get the sap on your skin, as it's an irritant.

CREATE COMPOSITION

Composition in this context means the art of grouping plants, planters, furniture and other features together within a space. Basically, it's what we as designers do all the time – paint the picture, fill the canvas and create the scene. It's not easy to explain, as it basically comes down to personal taste and the 'eye' of the designer, but it's essentially about drawing on surrounding materials, colours or textures to inspire your composition, ensuring it fits well into the space, so there is consistency and cohesion with what's around it.

When composing a table of interesting objects, odd numbers often work best, so keep groupings of plants and pots to threes and fives. You could also use pairs of objects to create structure, and then soften the look slightly by using odd numbers of other objects. Weave a common thread throughout the composition; for example, you might use a variety of different succulents or a collection of old vintage pots.

Apart from specially bred new cultivars and hybrids, most plants have been around since the dawn of time. It's how you put them together that creates the mood and makes an individual garden. I like to layer different kinds of foliage together to create interest and mood; it's in the subtle contrast of texture, form and colour that the magic happens. Even if you're just layering three plants together in a large planter on a roof terrace, composition is key.

Think about how a courtyard will looked when viewed from inside; don't forget to create interest in different areas of the garden space. You want to draw the eye to the foreground as well as the back and sides of the space.

This moody and very formal composition relies heavily on symmetry; note the use of the mirror to reflect surrounding views out of the terrace.

Combine planters of different sizes and shapes – tall, narrow, medium, or low and squat. Use repetition in the pots to give structure, and then contrast this with something a little more freeform. In this image you can see that the three tall cylinders planted with coral form of common jade give structure to the balcony, then we have layered another row of planters and objects of varying sizes, with varying foliage, in front.

Layers of plants at different heights help to contain and define a harbourside entertaining area.

Here a sleek, contemporary planter looks great next to an old terracotta water jar I found in Sri Lanka. The large ribbed pot at the back completes the picture.

This cool, leafy courtyard is composed of various points of interest – different foliage textures of giant strelitzia, kentia palm and bamboo, and objects such as hanging planters, lanterns and our marble tulip urns.

In the store we create compositions of different planters and objects to show people how to get a great result.

CHAPTER 2

Small Spaces

Our gardens and outdoor spaces are becoming smaller as more and more of us are living in the inner city where, if we have a garden at all, it is a small courtyard or balcony. Small spaces are very unforgiving, because everything is on show all at once. In a larger garden, the odd plant that is sick or not performing can be hidden by healthier, flourishing specimens. On a balcony, one dead plant will stick out like dogs' balls; there is no room for error, or plants that don't perform, or something that clashes or is the wrong shape or size.

So how do you approach small space garden design? What techniques can you employ to transform a harsh space into a verdant, restful and stylish retreat? Here are some examples of smaller spaces I have worked in. Admittedly, some of them are on the grander side of small, but I hope they provide some inspiration so you can set about creating your own outdoor haven.

Rooftop Garden in Rose Bay

OPPOSITE Coral form of common jade in a low woodfired bowl on the right. The spiky sotol in its recycled rubber pot provides a strong contrast in the corner.

ABOVE We chose clean lines and contemporary furniture.

THE CHALLENGE

This sun-drenched rooftop garden has an enviable position, sitting high on a hill above glorious Sydney Harbour. It's all about the view here. We just needed to frame it carefully, and it was crying out for some Garden Life personality.

The owner sought our help to create an entertainment space that flowed out from the living areas of her stylish penthouse. It's great to have a client who values her vast exterior space (about 200 square metres) as much as her interior. The challenge was to create intimacy and interest, yet still retain the expansive feeling, without cluttering it with anything unnecessary. Originally hailing from a small Greek island, our client loves nothing more than to gather friends and family together round a table to break bread and share stories.

The generous size of the rooftop meant we could integrate an outdoor seating and dining area with a large table for entertaining. Once we worked out where to place the lounging and eating areas, it was simply a case of seeing how to introduce softening focal points and some privacy.

Like the Australian Film, Television and Radio School rooftop (see the photograph on page 78) this space was completely barren, reflective and harsh in the extreme, consisting of little more than an expanse of pavers and balustrade. This meant we needed plants which love a sunny, open aspect, and could cope with the beating sun and exposed nature of the site. Starting with a plant palette of succulents, tough shrubs and textured conifers, we set about devising a scheme to create a minimalist garden that still had softness, interest and impact.

WHAT WE DID

We placed a series of simple, low contemporary bowls massed with succulents along the front of the terrace. The slick, polished concrete bowls are large enough to grab your attention and make an impact, but low enough so as not to obstruct the view. The **COTYLEDONS** we used are tough, versatile little numbers, that thrive in this position. The kitsch, orange, bell-like flowers pop up above the foliage in early autumn. For privacy at either boundary, we planted hedges of **CHINESE JUNIPER** (*Juniperus chinensis* 'Kaizuka', also called 'Keteleeri') under-planted with *Pittosporum* 'Miss Muffet', in large, lightweight troughs. We planted massed compact **COMMON JADE** (*Crassula ovata*) in lower troughs to define the left-hand boundary.

In each corner of the terrace we created interesting compositions of specimen plants, including clusters of **CORAL FORM OF COMMON JADE** (*Crassula ovata* 'Gollum'), *Kalanchoe orgyalis* 'Copper Spoons' and the very architectural **PONYTAIL PALM** (*Beaucarnea recurvata*). **RUSH-LEAF BIRD OF PARADISE** (*Strelitzia juncea*) provided striking colour and strong foliage,

This space before was barren, reflective and harsh in the extreme.

and we under-planted it with flowering **WHITE ICE PLANT** (*Lampranthus* spp.). These plants, with their different foliage, combine well, and are all ideally suited to this exposed, sun-drenched site, requiring very little water or maintenance.

We selected planters with a wide range of finishes – everything from polished concrete, galvanised steel with industrial oxide paint, to hand-bolted recycled rubber, wood-fired ceramic and bronze volcanic glazing. It's all about finding the right balance between contrasting textures, grouping them together to create consistency, then installing a random selection to create friction and interest.

We also removed the bollard lighting. It was in the wrong place, for starters, and the table-high, stainless steel posts were far too obtrusive. We installed recessing LED light into the paving, softly highlighting the troughs on either side and creating focal points in each corner. The lighting is now discreet but effective.

This rooftop garden is now a slick, sexy and vibrant space, with lots of colour and texture contrast, and soft and showy foliage in a prized position. What could be better?

Our client told me, 'When I come home, it's like a breath of fresh air – I feel like I have the most beautiful view in the world. The garden is the most beautiful addition to the apartment by far . . . a seamless extension of the house, where I can lie back and read in privacy, surrounded by beautifully textured pots and plants that flower all year round. I have always enjoyed alfresco dining, and now I love to enjoy a meal with my family out here around the table.'

CLOCKWISE FROM LEFT

A four-legged friend and a bowl massed with tough, versatile cotyledons.

Coral form of common jade in a wood-fired bowl gives great texture, contrasting with the clean lines.

The architectural leaves and flowers of the rush-leaf bird of paradise provide striking colour and strong foliage.

The carefully selected plants and containers create personality and a sense of intimacy in this stunning location.

Courtyard in Paddington

OPPOSITE I bought these beautifully detailed Turkish tiles from Marea (for more on her, see pages 197–198) and used them as the focal point in this leafy Paddington courtyard.

ABOVE Olive, resplendent in front of the composition of Indian jali screens and wall-mounted foliage.

THE CHALLENGE

The owners called us in to help with their small garden in Paddington. They had a very large (four-legged) problem – their beloved Great Dane Olive, a complete mother of a hound, with massive, garden-stomping paws. They certainly win the prize for having the largest dog in the smallest garden. The combination of big feet, huge, cowpat-sized poos and a shady situation was turning their tiny lawn into one big mess! The owners told me they wanted an oasis – lush, green plants, colour and a sense of inner-city jungle.

WHAT WE DID

The solution here was to plant some larger perennials and create a micro-jungle that the gentle giant can wander around without squashing everything. The garden is now an organised chaos of architectural foliage, softened with looser forms and evolving bits and bobs that survive against the odds.

First, we solved a privacy problem caused by a neighbour's recent renovation by planting a clump of bamboo which the owners have become particularly fond of. He says, 'The bamboo forest grows while you watch, and its gentle sway in the breeze is relaxing, like being on holidays. It really is a haven, and friends who visit are always surprised at how cool it seems'.

We planted a large **GYMEA LILY** (*Doryanthes excelsa*) in the middle of the garden, and next to this strong structure we used the old-fashioned, nana-like **CANE BEGONIA** (*Begonia coccinea*). I love how it looks against the sword-like Gymea lily leaves. We used the stunning **BROMELIAD EMPRESS OF BRAZIL** (*Alcantarea imperialis* 'Rubra') to provide further strong foliage form. We have experimented with various kinds of 'dog-proof' lower foliage, and the ones which seem to survive best are **BRAZILIAN WALKING IRIS** (*Neomarica gracilis*) and the sturdy **GIANT MONDO GRASS** (*Ophiopogon jaburan*). Olive manages to travel through these without doing too much damage. We also planted some romantic greenery, including the delightfully scented and ornamental **CARDAMOM** (*Alpinia nutans*) and a mass of **STAR JASMINE** (*Trachelospermum jasminoides*) to frame a stunning, ornate Turkish tiled panel. **ELK HORN FERN** (*Platycerium bifurcatum*) and masses of **SPANISH MOSS** (*Tillandsia usneoides*) hanging from the trees add to the atmosphere.

All the plants seem to co-exist happily in this tiny oasis; indeed I don't think I have ever used so many different species in such a small space, but it all seems to work, and Olive now loves to hang out in her own jungle!

Up towards the house, we recently refreshed the space by installing a composition of Indian jali screens on the wall, along with brass planters and several **BIRD'S NEST FERN** (*Asplenium australasicum*), and a couple of years ago we helped the owners establish a herb and vegie garden on their garage rooftop. Using a couple of large prefab oval beds and some good-quality soil, we managed to create a little bit of biodiversity for them, enabling them to garden together as a family. They have had some killer tomatoes, loads of mint (as it can overtake everything!) and one lone cabbage that wouldn't have made the grade in a veg shop but was apparently tasty all the same.

ABOVE I love how much is going on in this small space. We set out to create a full, layered, richly textured courtyard – the sword-like leaves of the Gymea lily provide structure and stop it from looking too disorganised.

BOTTOM LEFT Soft new shoots of bamboo planted to solve a privacy issue.

BOTTOM RIGHT Lovely, old-fashioned blooms of the cane begonia.

CREATE VERTICAL SPACE

When you have only limited floor space, it's essential to consider what vertical space is available. It might be at either end of a balcony, a garden fence or just the side of a building.

CLIMBING PLANTS

One solution is climbing plants, but beware, as I have seen far too many failed climbers in pots. If you are going to use pots, make sure you choose large ones with reliable irrigation. Climbing plants will often grow well at first, then dry out as they become pot-bound, making the entire wall look dead. To avoid this happening, be prepared to re-pot them every few years, and make sure they are kept well-watered.

STAR JASMINE (*Trachelospermum jasminoides*) has always been a great climber for a sunny wall, and it will grow wherever there is a support. The self-supporting BOSTON IVY (*Parthenocissus tricuspidata*) on a rendered boundary or house wall is very stylish and looks terrific in winter when the stems are bare.

We use CREEPING FIG (*Ficus pumila*) a lot as it's a versatile climber, which will blanket ugly fences or harsh walls (no wires required) and grow in full sun or shade. It will need clipping four times a year to stop it becoming overgrown (it has a bad name for this).

SCREENS

Consider installing a screen on the wall as a feature, or for privacy. There are a plethora of laser-cut screens now available in many different styles and finishes, so you should be able to find something you like, whether it is a screen with an earthy, rusty finish or a slick, powder-coated colour that will blend with an interior colour scheme.

I love using our Indian jali screens to create a patchwork pattern on slick, rendered walls. We bring them in from Rajasthan, and they are full of character, warmth and history. They work in both a classic and contemporary space; it all depends on how they are configured on a wall. Old Indian doors can also add weight and warmth in the right space, it's just a question of personal taste and what you are drawn towards.

You can also use the plants themselves to create a screen.

HANGING POTS

Hanging pots are useful in tight corners and other hard-to-plant areas and can really liven up a small space especially.

GREEN WALLS

Green walls, or vertical gardens, have become quite fashionable, although the cost of bespoke systems and their maintenance can be beyond the home gardener. You could try creating your own green walls using climbers and then installing epiphytic plants on the wall or fence, as long as you have enough light. STAG AND ELK HORN FERN (*Platycerium bifurcatum*) are perfect for this; try staggering a few on a wall covered with CREEPING FIG (*Ficus pumila*).

OTHER IDEAS

A good solution for making new timber fences look more attractive is to paint them a dark colour and grow a climber up them (depending on the light conditions). Dark colours help green to stand out, so don't be afraid to use something like charcoal – it will help make your boundary fence disappear and really show off your foliage. Please don't ever use lattice! A smarter alternative is simply to have some horizontal timber boards mounted and painted in place of the dreadful stuff.

There are many different tiles and kinds of stone cladding available, and these can add interest and also link an exterior wall to an interior scheme. Be careful to avoid fads though – there are lots of walls of stacked stone veneer around town now looking very dated. If you use tiles or stone, keep it classic and simple.

The simplest way to create a green wall is to use a climber – this fragrant star jasmine in full flower on the wall at Point Piper really frames the archway (see pages 12–27).

Don't be afraid to make a bold statement, even in a small courtyard such as the one in Paddington (see pages 98–101).

Hanging planters of succulents soften the horizontal timber lines in the courtyard in Newtown (see pages 104–107).

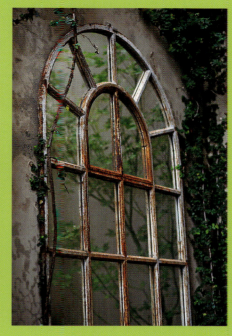

Mirrors can create another dimension in any space. This antique French mirror fits in perfectly at Point Piper, adding depth and light to a dark corner (see pages 12–27).

The upright habit of black bamboo works well when floor space is limited.

Create interest on a dull wall by using a composition of different screens as we did in Paddington (see pages 98–101).

Hand-made Indian jalis are a nice soft option for decorating stark walls. We used a series of nine in the townhouse in Walsh Bay (see pages 108–111).

Courtyard in Newtown

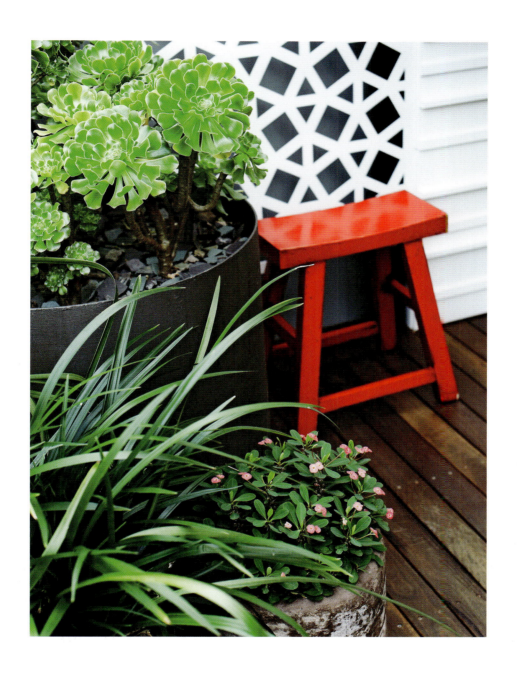

OPPOSITE Faux-bamboo sofa underneath hanging planters filled with epiphyllum. Dave Edmonds makes these planters locally (for more on him, see page 185).

ABOVE This red stool adds a burst of contrasting colour to the bright foliage of the succulent Aeonium.

THE CHALLENGE

When I first saw it, this courtyard was truly dreadful. It belonged to a newly built terrace house, and the outdoor space, which was about 6 metres wide by 10 metres deep, consisted of two boundary walls, a roller door and a concrete floor, facing directly due west. There was nothing remotely attractive about it – it was just a concrete cube. Oh, I almost forgot the air conditioner extraction unit pumping out hot air directly outside the cheap, developer-installed French doors, where the house stopped at the back door of the kitchen.

The clients' brief was to create another living space, by expanding the compact kitchen and dining area out into the space beyond. She wanted extra space for lounging and relaxing, and he wanted an integrated barbecue and space to keep the drinks cool in summer.

WHAT WE DID

We had a good budget to work with here, enabling us to address both the big picture and all the small details that really matter in a confined space. Our clients and their excitable bull terrier, Roxy, were as excited as I was about turning the space around.

We started by moving all the services to the back of the space. We replaced the French doors with slick bi-folds, which created a better connection between inside and outside. We rebuilt the existing pergola, fully lining it with timber battening to soften the harsh sun and create some privacy on either side. To really create a seamless link to the kitchen, we installed a deck of spotted gum to extend outside at the same level as the kitchen floor. We built an integrated barbecue and bar fridge down one side of the new entertaining space, and we designed cupboards which matched the units in the kitchen.

The car space was non-negotiable; we just had to find a solution to separate and define the area. Our in-house-designed Geo screen was just the thing, visually diffusing the car space, and wrapping around the side wall, hiding the unsightly relocated services, air-conditioning unit and rubbish bins. It's made of a series of geometric shapes, and custom sizable so it works well in most small spots. The spaces are just the right size to provide a good screen, without blocking out the sunlight.

Planting in a small, enclosed space like this needed to be soft and bold to make an impact. It also needed to be BIG. We planted a contrasting collection of softening foliage in a group of galvanised cylinders. The **GIANT BIRD OF PARADISE** (*Strelitzia nicolai*) provided the large foliage, and we layered that with succulents, **GIANT MONDO GRASS** (*Ophiopogon jaburan*) and other contrasting foliage. We hung a collection of Dave Edmonds' hanging pots, planted with **EPIPHYLLUM**

Our brief was to turn this concrete cube into an outdoor living space.

and **MISTLETOE CACTUS** (*Rhipsalis baccifera*) succulents under the pergola, to add some texture.

Finally, we added some well-placed, faux bamboo outdoor furniture in canary yellow to contribute to the fresh feel, and we used the clients' existing stools to complete the picture.

I'm really proud of this little courtyard, because the transformation was so huge. I think the expression 'outdoor room' is a little over-used, although here we literally created another space for the house, seamlessly connected to the inside.

CLOCKWISE FROM LEFT

The laser-cut Geo screening diffuses the car space and provides a backdrop to a lush corner containing giant bird of paradise, Aeonium, jade and giant mondo grass.

Mother-in-law's tongue looks striking in one of our recycled rubber pots.

This cheeky fella has become an unofficial Garden Life mascot!

At the end of the outdoor kitchen sits a collection of foliage, including a dragon tree.

Townhouse in Walsh Bay

OPPOSITE This internal atrium garden is literally another room within the house. The coastal banksia provides scale and movement, and softens the two-storey space.

ABOVE The linear form and precise placement of the sandstone make the tiny space seem much larger.

THE CHALLENGE

It's very affirming to get repeat work from a client, and I was touched when this couple asked us to help them refresh the outdoor spaces and atrium we had transformed ten years earlier. While large, sprawling gardens take time to mature, when your garden is a room in your house it will need overhauling after a decade.

This contemporary, four-level, inner-city family home reflects the industrial history of the Sydney wharf area, with its hard-edged, raw finishes of glass, steel and concrete. The 5 by 3 metre atrium is surrounded on three sides by glass, and because it dominates the main living areas of the house, it really has the potential to enhance the home. The plants we use here not only offer a beautiful aesthetic, but also affect the microclimate within the home by providing a buffer to the sunlight and heat in the height of summer.

The atrium extends for two levels of the house, so it can be seen from many different angles. These internal open spaces are really tricky, and need to be carefully thought out. All the basic design tips apply here – you need to consider scale, composition, texture, contrasts, vertical space – and sexy pots! Spaces like this, which are becoming more and more common in contemporary architecture, can make or break the feel of a home. Well-designed, they can bring great natural light right into the middle of a house, but often they resemble a barren, reflective shocker with a sad palm tree as an afterthought in the corner.

When we first created the space, we placed three large, woven willow panels on the massive rear wall, a substantial black bamboo in a large, mint-green pot, some long pieces of slate on the floor, and pads of timber deck, running in different directions on the floor. It was a simple composition, using different textures, but it really worked. It was just looking a little tired – and the willow panels were on their way back to their maker!

WHAT WE DID

As you walk up the stairs to the living area, the back wall of the atrium is very dominant, so we had to make good use of this large vertical surface – it demanded something special. We went with a series of nine handmade iron jali screens from India. Their delicate texture and intricate pattern soften the bland wall, and the repetition keeps it strong and bold.

We needed an advanced tree to anchor the courtyard and provide the necessary shade, and we settled on a **COASTAL BANKSIA** (*Banksia integrifolia*). Its natural habit and slightly wild aesthetic appealed to me and the owners, and I hand-selected just the right specimen at the nursery on one of my buying trips. A second, smaller specimen helped it to look at home, and we planted both in a custom-built, large

The series of nine handmade intricate Indian jalis soften the bland rendered wall.

amoeba-shaped planter painted with Murobond Bridge Paint, reflecting the industrial nature of the architecture. In the opposite corner we mass-planted a second pot, finished the same way, with **CAST-IRON PLANT** (*Aspidistra elatior*). Finally, I selected an old Turkish tree trunk, to introduce an earthy feel, and planted it with a specimen of **ALOE** (*Aloe* x *spinosissima*). This produced a basic composition of three contrasting elements in the space.

We also planted a series of large specimens of **FIRESTICKS** (*Euphorbia tirucalli*) at the front of the house, to reduce the impact of the scorching afternoon sun the house receives in the summer months.

For the flooring we used large slabs of Sydney sandstone cut to size, with soft brown pea gravel in between. Once again, this was a combination of a natural texture with a slick layout, the rough with the smooth, the organic and rigid, all combining to create a harmonious result. The orientation of the stone enhances the sense of space and creates interest.

The execution of this installation involved precision planning by big brother Mick, our installation guru, as all deliveries had to be craned on site and the jali screens had to be rust-proofed with epoxy paint, then installed by a professional hanger. All of this takes time and patience, and Mick's wealth of experience helped it all to go smoothly.

I'm really chuffed with the end result. It looks natural and understated, yet chic, slick and really effective. I'm looking forward to watching it develop.

CLOCKWISE, FROM TOP

Texture is important here – the old Turkish tree trunk planted with aloe offsets the strong lines of the sandstone flooring.

The spaghetti-like leaves of the rhipsalis spill down from the terrace into the courtyard.

Installation logistics are often difficult when you are working in confined spaces!

CREATE SCALE

To my mind, scale is possibly the most important element of garden design. It becomes especially important when you are working with small spaces. The most common misconception about small spaces is that you must use small elements within them. PLEASE DO THE OPPOSITE!! Be brave and use the largest pieces you practically can. Whilst it is important to leave yourself some room just to 'be' in the space, I urge you to go for the bold gesture. Use large-scale pieces to trick the eye into thinking the space is larger than it appears. Smaller pieces have the opposite effect.

If you are laying a deck in a small space, use an extra-wide timber, and lay the timber so it runs along the shortest length of the space. Your eye will follow the line of the timber, making the deck appear longer or wider than it is. In terms of plant size, I'd much rather one large planter with a stunning plant than a few smaller insignificant pots. Better still, have three big pots all together. (Do remember to take into account door widths, stairs, lifts and access issues, which are often forgotten!)

This is a good example of how to use large-scale pieces in a confined area. The rear garden was dominated by an imposing garage wall and was crying out for a strong focal point, so we installed a massive planter, 150 centimetres in diameter, and planted it with a super-advanced specimen of tree aloe.

Make sure, when you are choosing pots, that the pot is the right scale for the plant. It's pointless having a lovely, big planter with a tiny plant in it – it's much better to spend a little more so you have something with immediate impact.

At the townhouse in Walsh Bay (see pages 108–111) we used one big, custom-made planter as the centrepiece in the tiny atrium, adding structure, impact and drama.

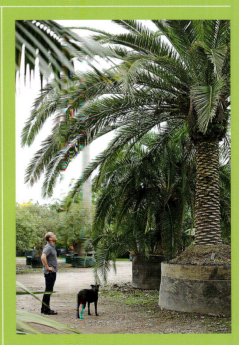

In the middle of Geoffrey Bawa's garden at Lunuganga in Sri Lanka (see pages 91–94) he planted a magnificent frangipani which takes centre stage and dominates the view from the house – it's a great use of scale.

In the driveway at Bellevue Hill (see pages 34–47) we installed four large contemporary bowls, planted with advanced cycads, which we placed on plinths to sit them just above the box hedge.

These Canary Island date palms are a perfect example of imported scale. One of these in your garden could immediately solve a privacy issue, or just provide an amazing feature from the get-go. These can be craned into confined spaces – they are not just for large gardens.

Garden in Rozelle

OPPOSITE The giant bird of paradise gives this sheltered spot a tropical-resort feel.

ABOVE The planting needed to soften the straight lines of the glass-sided lap pool.

THE CHALLENGE

There are few people I know who are as infatuated with swimming as these two, so when they decided to install a lap pool in their small urban garden no one was surprised.

When they first moved into their lovely weatherboard cottage, the garden had a formal, rigid feel, with a big koi carp pond down the side surrounded with some fake sandstone pavers laid on a forty-five degree angle (whoever thought that was a good idea ought to be shot!). The owners quickly engaged architects to design a slick, glass-sided pool to replace the carp pond, using polished concrete for the pool floor. This very contemporary pool contrasted superbly with the warmth of the more traditional cottage.

The owners approached us to help create an oasis, an escape where they could hang out with their two gorgeous kids and forget they were in the middle of the city.

One of them explained what they wanted like this. 'We try to make our home better than any holiday destination, as you spend most of your time at home. Having stayed at high-end resorts, we wanted the same feeling for our own garden. As we have two young children, staying at home is such a pleasure, a treat even. This is what we set out to create – a holiday destination at home.'

WHAT WE DID

Glass, water and concrete are all rather cold, hard elements, and we needed to soften up the renovation to create the right balance between the pool, the house and the garden. Major lush foliage was required in the two small pockets of garden at either end of the pool.

We set about creating a rich, tropically layered scheme. Being big fans of the GIANT BIRD OF PARADISE (*Strelitzia nicolai*), we planted a few specimens to soften the dominating boundary wall. It's a great plant for softening this type of area. Be sure to give it a sheltered spot, away from strong winds which can tear the leaves and leave it looking scrappy. At the other end of the pool we dropped in some advanced BANGALOW PALM (*Archontophoenix cunninghamiana*), and placed a large FRANGIPANI (*Plumeria rubra* var *acutifolia*) at the top of the stairs, above the front gate (I love seeing that tree everywhere in Sydney summers).

We used slick, white cylinders planted with large FIDDLE-LEAF FIGS (*Ficus lyrata*) to add a 'wow' factor next to the barbecue, and repeated this upstairs on the balcony. White BUTTERFLY GINGER (*Hedychium coronarium*) and ELEPHANT EARS (*Alocasia macrorrhizos*) provided the middle layer of lushness. For the lower level of planting, we used mass plantings of BRAZILIAN WALKING IRIS (*Neomarica gracilis*), PERSIAN SHIELD (*Strobilanthes gossypinus*) and good old AUSTRALIAN NATIVE VIOLET (*Viola hederacea*) to add further softness.

The owners now describe the garden as their sanctuary, far away from the hustle and bustle of city life. Their two children love racing about on their scooters, and are very much at home in the pool.

One of them told me, 'Before the new garden, we rarely used the space. Now we are out there almost every day of the week, and even more on weekends. We often open up all the windows and doors, turn up the music, crack open a Corona and feel like we could be at the Chateau Marmont in LA.'

CLOCKWISE FROM LEFT

The fashionable fiddle-leaf fig looks amazing in this slick white cylinder.

Angus having fun in the pool

The lime green ceramic pot contrasts well with the rush-leaf bird of paradise

Richly planted tropical beds at either end of the pool provide the resort feel that the owners were looking for.

CREATE

CREATE WITH FURNITURE AND ACCESSORIES

These days, there are many interesting bits and pieces around which can enhance our outdoor spaces. Outdoor lanterns, brass candlesticks and beeswax candles can all add to the look of a space, and add another dimension to an occasion.

You can accessorise to make a space your own using any objects which mean something to you – pebbles, driftwood or shells collected from a beach, old pieces of stone or sculpture, seed capsules or even animal skulls (for the more adventurous!).

Twenty or thirty years ago outdoor furniture comprised the white PVC outdoor setting by the pool, and a treated pine picnic table and benches to eat at. Now, happily, there are all kinds of different colours, textures and options available for dining, lounging and relaxing. We're not even limited to tables and chairs – we have beanbags, outdoor swings, coffee tables – basically the same number of options we have for indoor furniture.

Think carefully about your choice of outdoor furniture. I suggest that you approach buying outdoor furniture in the same way that you would buy indoor pieces; basically, you get what you pay for. Inexpensive pieces are likely to collapse, fade or rust in a couple of years.

A common misconception about outdoor furniture is that everything has to match. Forget that – you don't always need to use a matching set of table and chairs. A slick table can look great surrounded by mismatched chairs.

When you are selecting wooden furniture, try to use timber from sustainably managed forests when possible – head to www.goodwoodguide.org for reference.

We used bright Missoni print cushions which really stand out against the slick, polished concrete floor in the Rozelle garden. The crisp white furniture by Richard Schultz also suits the restrained nature of the garden perfectly.

Italian designer Paola Lenti uses traditional craft techniques like knitting with marine-grade rope to create stunning contemporary yet soft furniture.

You can use colourful outdoor furniture to add brightness to an otherwise neutral space. Here we used a fresh, green outdoor setting to contrast with the otherwise natural, earthy courtyard.

Outdoor furniture today looks very similar to that inside our homes, with outdoor rugs, coffee tables and ottomans.

Here we used antique brass candlesticks, a ceramic bowl by Dave Edmonds massed with seedpods, and our hanging planters – together they add bucketloads of personality and charm.

Simple potted succulents look great on tables.

Outdoor lanterns help to create great atmosphere at night.

Townhouse in Darling Point

OPPOSITE A soft jade hedge under-planted with 'Silver Falls' frames the view from the rooftop terrace.

ABOVE Pool water feature designed by interior designer, Claire Rendall.

THE CHALLENGE

Once again, our brief here was to create a garden which felt like an ultra-high-end resort – a sanctuary with a colonial feel. The owners had a beautiful collection of objects from their world travels, which the garden scheme had to incorporate.

One of the owners told me, 'We want something different, something that comes alive and captures the imagination – a place where we can sit, gaze and contemplate the wonders of it all.'

The garden is made up of a series of small spaces which surround the home. Although we needed to approach each space separately, we also had to ensure they were connected.

The inside of the house was finished to an incredibly high standard, including a large amount of custom-made items freighted here from the UK. The garden had to marry perfectly with this sumptuous renovation, and we collaborated heavily with the interior designer, Claire Rendall, to ensure that the interior and exterior were cohesive. Claire had strong ideas about what she wanted to see in the garden – rich layering and contrasting textures within the plant palette, with lots of flowers and soft, lush foliage, like a luxe subtropical resort. We worked hard to produce a planting scheme which achieved the look she wanted.

WHAT WE DID

The house sits on three levels, with a large wrap-around terrace off the ground floor and a generous terrace off the upstairs bedrooms. The available planting space was minimal, so most of the garden was in planters or built-in raised beds. The generous budget allowed us free rein with the finishes and materials. The walls, floors and planter boxes were covered in cream Italian limestone, and we chose to contrast and soften this with rich, darker tones of bronze, brass and other metallic colours for the planters, urns and ornamentation.

We decided to go hard on the planting to help soften the dominant built form, choosing a combination of soft, gentle, layered plants and strong architectural plants. We used ELEPHANT EARS (*Alocasia macrorrhizos*) and GIANT BIRD OF PARADISE (*Strelitzia nicolai*) to make up the larger foliage, and integrated some aromatic, ornamental CARDAMOM (*Alpinia nutans*) and BRAZILIAN WALKING IRIS (*Neomarica gracilis*) for lower interest. We planted masses of BRONZE-FOLIAGED BROMELIADS (*Billbergia* 'Halleluja') in hand-carved, tulip urns, and large palms in our own bullet bowls, which we covered in a snakeskin finish. To provide some privacy, we planted long troughs of COMMON JADE (*Crassula ovata*) in a soft, organic hedge under-planted with *Dichondra argentea* 'Silver Falls', a very adaptable groundcover which loves to trail down and soften the sides of planters and bowls.

At the front of the property, facing the street, we clumped advanced specimens of the striking MAURITIUS HEMP (*Furcraea foetida*), a superb, indestructible plant which doubles as a security screen. We used a mass of the groundcover BUSH MORNING GLORY (*Convolvulus sabatius* 'Two Moons'), so named because its flowers are two shades of blue on the same plant, to soften the base. We also included some more traditional, cottage-style plants, such as FRENCH LAVENDER (*Lavandula dentata*) and SILVER SPURFLOWER (*Plectranthus argentatus*), and even some NEW GUINEA IMPATIENS (*Impatiens* New Guinea Hybrids) for colour in the shadier spots. Claire was horrified when confronted with these – very pedestrian indeed, she thought (although she wanted us to include common AGAPANTHUS (*Agapanthus praecox*) in the scheme; in the UK these are seen as very exotic, whereas here we see them on our highways!). In my defence, I have to say that NEW GUINEA IMPATIENS are handsome, non-weedy forms of impatiens, with large vibrant pink or orange flowers and striking green to bronze leaves.

A pair of huge cast bronze striated urns adds to the sense of decadence when you first enter the garden, and we planted these with big specimens of CARDBOARD PALM (*Zamia furfuracea*), whose stiff brown-green leaves give the plant its common name. Upstairs, off the bedroom, we planted a variegated form of MAURITIUS HEMP (*Furcraea foetida*) in an antique Indian brass planter, and once again used a series of bronzed troughs massed with COMMON JADE (*Crassula ovata*) underplanted with *Dichondra argentea* 'Silver Falls' to soften the balustrade.

It's now a garden that the owners love to look out on and 'be' in. One of them told me, 'We take such delight in knowing that we have created something special in terms of outcome. Our home is a townhouse with a terrace on each level, but it doesn't feel like that as we have created a flowing garden which we enjoy and which doesn't need a lot of maintenance. We simply love spending time there – it is truly magical, vibrant and alive.'

The end result is a little over-the-top in some ways (in contrast with much of our other work) and I love that. It's really satisfying to be able to develop different schemes to suit different clients, and essential to approach each job with our clients' needs in the forefront of our minds. At the end of the day, our job as designers is to work to the clients' brief, to create the garden they want, for them to enjoy.

CLOCKWISE FROM LEFT

We chose a combination of architectual plants and softer, layered ones.

Silver spurflower spills over and softens the garden wall, with elephant ears in the background above an antique Indian marble piece.

A lovely old sandstone window frame in between a giant bird of paradise and a frangipani adds character to the slick limestone wall.

One of our hand-carved marble tulip planters massed with bromeliads.

A striking specimen of variegated Mauritius hemp in an old copper pot I found on my travels in Rajasthan.

CREATE USING POTS

You can use pots in gardens of any size, but they are particularly useful in smaller gardens, where a well-selected planter or two is a sure-fire way to transform a small space. There are endless sizes and shapes – from a small herb trough on a window ledge or a hand-thrown ceramic hanging planter, to a monster pot two metres in diameter. You can basically grow plants in anything that holds potting mix and has a drainage hole – it's just a matter of finding the right planter that works in your space.

Here are a few things to bear in mind:
- choose functional pots for the framework, and contrast with a hero piece which will act as a focal point
- use a pot that is size-appropriate for your space (see pages 44–45 on scale) – generally speaking, the bigger the better
- spend your money in visible areas, and use a less expensive option if the planter is concealed, for example in a service area
- use clusters of small pots planted with interesting plants to make a collector's table
- remember to allow enough room in the pot for the plant to grow for a few years. So, if your plant comes in a plastic pot 30 centimetres in diameter, ideally choose a pot of at least 50 centimetres in diameter
- the main thing is to select a piece that resonates with you, one that you love.

There are a few things to remember when planting in pots. First, pots dry out more quickly than gardens, so ensure really thirsty plants such as bamboos and ferns, for example, are given special attention. Next, raise the pot off the ground with high-density rubber to allow for drainage and for air to circulate. Finally, use the best-quality Premium potting mix, which meets the Australian Standard – you get what you pay for, as it has better drainage, controlled release fertiliser and water-saving crystals.

The three tall white cylinder planters on page 125 are some of my favourites. Sleek and very cool, they provide the perfect frame for the MOTHER-IN-LAW'S TONGUE (*Sansevieria*). I also love the classic, graceful lines of the Indian hand-carved tulip planter massed with bromeliads at the townhouse in Darling Point (see the photograph on page 123).

At Bellevue Hill the clean lines of the contemporary charcoal bowls sit perfectly in a formal setting whether they add drama up the driveway, nestling by the pool or sitting on top of the barbecue (see the photograph on page 35).

I always love seeing the mad yellow pineapple planter when I visit Byron View Farm, it's perfect coupled with the PONYTAIL PALM (*Beaucarnea recurvata*) and just looks after itself.

This recycled rubber pot used to be a car tyre. Massed with bromeliads.

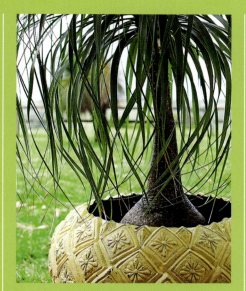

I love this mad vintage pineapple planter with its ponytail palm at Byron View Farm.

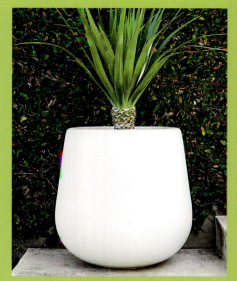

The slick lines of this contemporary vase make a striking home for this dragon tree.

This series of cylinders shows how well repetition works in a confined space.

Planters hand-knitted with marine-grade rope.

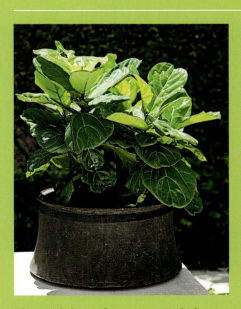

The simple lines of an antique Turkish planter frame this fiddle-leaf fig perfectly.

These copper vases are handmade locally from offcuts of copper pipes.

Simple, lightweight, narrow troughs add great structure and clean lines.

PART 2

Connect

Harvest 130

Share 150

Growing your own produce is a great way to connect more deeply with your garden – and your community. It's heart-warming to see the popularity of school programs like Stephanie Alexander's Kitchen Garden Program, and a plethora of home vegie gardening books, all of which have played a part in the revival of interest in growing more of the food we eat. If you have the space, start an edible garden in your own back or front yard. If you don't, think about banding together with a group of like-minded neighbours to start your own community garden, as we did in Redfern, with the James Street Reserve Community Garden.

For many reasons, starting with the fact that it is good for our health and for the environment, I believe we should all try to grow whatever food we can in our available outdoor space. It might mean transforming the so-called 'nature' strips outside the front of our houses (an ironic name, given that most of them are weed-covered pieces of brown grass; not much nature happening there!), or simply growing a handful of herbs and vegies in the sunniest spot in the garden.

Having a go and growing your own isn't for everybody – it does require a little effort, although, as they say, you reap what you sow. Instead of going out to clip the hedge or prune the roses, you can go out and connect with your soil by planting seeds, staking the tomatoes, watering and picking a salad for dinner.

I'm not talking about becoming totally self-sufficient, with three pigs and a sheep in the backyard, but you could start with a rosemary bush, or use thyme as a groundcover you can pick when roasting a chicken. Flat-leaf parsley and rocket are so useful, and easy to grow amongst other plants. Try planting some radish seeds with your kids or friends' kids, like my dad did with me; they will cherish the memory as I do, and you never know where it will lead. Just have a go and start growing something in your patch of ground, however small it is.

If you don't have the space in your own garden, you can get just as much enjoyment from a community garden, which has the added benefit of bringing people together. My involvement with the James Street Reserve Community Garden has really made me appreciate the importance of being part of a community. When I see people coming together and connecting in the space, and hear chatter between people who wouldn't usually meet, the social benefits are obvious. You can't underestimate the importance of projects like these, and the sense of connection and belonging they create.

CHAPTER 3

Harvest

I truly believe that the experience of growing food is a rich and rewarding one, which not only provides us with nourishing food, but also allows us to connect with each other. So many of our gardens are sterile, unproductive plots, but they have the potential to be fertile, nourishing spaces filled with fresh produce.

Here are some ideas about how to set up your own amazing edible garden, plus a look at how some enterprising individuals are producing homegrown fruit and vegies on a larger scale.

My Vegie Patch

One way for me to encourage clients, neighbours and local residents to integrate edibles into their own gardens is to set an example in my own garden to show how easy it is. There is absolutely nothing I find more satisfying than going outside to pick some fresh leaves for a simple salad, or cut some crisp rhubarb stems for a crumble or pie. We needn't be running out to the shops to buy this stuff – it's ludicrous!

We recently moved house and inherited a sunny, north-east-facing front garden – perfect for growing food, apart from the fact that it was one big slab of concrete! We quickly ripped up the old 'Greek lawn' and started to convert the 12 square metres of tiled terror into a productive patch. After we removed the broken slabs of masonry, we carefully sifted through and removed debris and old building rubble hidden under the slab from a renovation in the '60s. We then added new soil, bringing in topsoil and composted organic matter to return some goodness to the soil. My new next-door neighbour, Julian, kindly donated some slabs of sandstone, which I used as stepping stones, lending the space some earthy structure.

The vegie garden receives only the morning sun, but so far it is enough to produce plentiful crops of fennel, rhubarb, Cos lettuce, rocket and massive amounts of flat-leaf parsley. Globe artichokes are currently taking centre stage, although I think they may want more sun to actually produce a crop; we shall soon see.

To ensure the garden still has some structure and definition, I have planted a large, clipped **PLUM PINE** (*Podocarpus elatus*) in the corner, as well as a simple ball of **JAPANESE BOX** (*Buxus microphylla* var. *japonica*). As I have mentioned before, for me, it is essential to strike the right balance between order and chaos in any space, and the vegie garden can look as wild as it wants to as long as it is grounded by the restrained shapes of the topiary.

One unexpected consequence of creating our edible garden is the steady stream of folk who stop for a chat when I'm out in the space, offering advice or just to tell me how much they enjoy passing by and seeing what is happening. It's been a terrific way for me to acquaint myself with the locals, and bolsters the sense of living together in a community. How good would it be if we all grew just a few things in our gardens and then bartered what we didn't need for something that we did? A neighbour in my old street had the biggest and bushiest rosemary ever, and encouraged everyone

OPPOSITE In my element – in my front garden you can see rhubarb, fennel, flat-leaf parsley, Vietnamese mint, artichoke, Cos lettuce, sorrel, rocket, borage and mustard greens. A clipped Japanese box gives good form.

ABOVE A random mix of foliage goodness viewed from the front.

BELOW Cos lettuce.

to come and pick some as and when required. I have now planted a bush that will hopefully provide the same abundance to my new street when it has matured. Living in the city, we can't grow all of the produce we need, but we can go a long way to becoming more self-sufficient and connecting with each other in the process.

Getting Started

The productive garden shouldn't be relegated to a corner of the backyard anymore; with city space at a premium, it's about growing food wherever the sunshine is. It can look just as good as it will taste! Our urban front gardens needn't look like sterile, mini-versions of Versailles, but can be rich, productive, diverse little pockets of goodness. It's one thing to create beautiful ornamental gardens, but even more satisfying to create stunning gardens that are productive as well.

Here is some basic advice about soil and a couple of other things to get you started on growing your own food, whatever space you have, whether it is a windowsill, balcony, small front yard or suburban garden. Do as much reading as you can, on the internet and elsewhere (I'll suggest a few books at the end of this chapter), then I urge you just to get out there and have a go!

SOIL

Where to start with soil? When you grow your own food, the quality of the end result is highly dependent on your soil quality. In simple terms, the healthier your soil, the healthier your fruit and vegies will be. One of the reasons why Quentin and Leslie from Kurrawong Organics (see pages 144–147) rest theirs for two years between crops is to give it a chance to recuperate. It's hard to do that in a domestic situation, but luckily we can cheat a little to improve the soil in our urban gardens.

It's all about the organic matter. By adding organic matter to your garden beds you increase the biological activity in the soil, attracting worms and healthy microorganisms, as well as improving the soil's aeration and its capacity to retain water. You also make it easier for the plants to absorb nutrients.

Generally speaking, Australian soils are based on either sand or clay, or varying proportions of both. Sandy soils tend to have good drainage, but their downside is that they don't hold nutrients or moisture well. By adding organic matter you solve both problems, as this enables nutrients to be absorbed by the plants and also aids moisture retention. Clay soils, on the other hand, retain moisture and nutrients very well, although they can be heavy due to poor drainage and aeration, leading to root rot and other problems. Adding organic matter to a heavy clay soil helps to break it up and allows air spaces to form. You need oxygen in your soil so that microorganisms can thrive and nutrient exchange can occur.

COMPOSTING AND WORM FARMS

Every home needs a compost bin or a worm farm – or both. If you use either you will not only be reducing landfill and saving the energy it takes to transport it, but also improving your own soil quality. It's one of the small, everyday things that we can do ourselves to make a difference to the environment.

Garden compost, made from broken-down kitchen scraps and garden waste, is an essential source of organic matter, and provides a rich supply of nutrients for the soil.

There are various kinds of compost bins and tumblers available – choose one that suits your space, and place it somewhere accessible in the garden.

ABOVE The best broom is a Tumut Millet broom, made right here in New South Wales!

OPPOSITE TOP Artichoke foliage – in the end there wasn't enough sun for these to do well.

OPPOSITE BOTTOM Rhubarb thrives here – it loves the sheltered position. We always had clumps of it in the garden when I was growing up.

Kids adore harvest time! Especially Amy, my niece.

To ensure good results with compost, there are a few simple rules to follow. First, compost should be a mixture of carbon and nitrogen (the carbon to nitrogen ratio should be around 25:1). The carbon comes from 'brown' material, like dead leaves, small twigs, straw and torn newspaper or cardboard, and the nitrogen comes from 'green' material, like kitchen scraps and lawn clippings. If your compost heap has too many kitchen scraps and lawn clippings it will become too wet, so you need the dead leaves and torn newspaper to balance this. Layer the heap, so that each time you add vegie peelings, you also add some torn cardboard or dead leaves as well.

Next, make sure that the compost gets the oxygen it needs. Buy a compost aerator (it looks like a giant corkscrew) from your local hardware store, and give your compost a weekly turn to keep some air in it. It takes about three months to make compost – when it is ready it will have a dark colour and a crumbly, consistent texture that smells sweet (if it smells like ammonia, it needs more carbon, so add dead leaves, torn newspaper or straw). Keen composters have two or even three bins. When one is full, they seal it and leave it for a few months to decompose, and use the second, then the third when the second is full.

If you live in an apartment or a small urban space and a compost bin isn't practical, then a worm farm is a must. Start with about 1000 worms and place them in a worm farm (available from your local hardware store), then feed them small amounts of kitchen scraps (well chopped) each day. As they munch their way through your scraps, the worms excrete a rich liquid which is stored in the bottom tray. You then dilute that on a 1:10 ratio and use it as a rich liquid manure to apply to your plants.

Worm farms are simple – there are just a few things to remember. First, keep the worms in the shade; cover with a hessian sack if you can find one. Next, don't include any citrus in your scraps as worms don't like the acidity. Finally, make sure the bottom tray has good drainage, and that liquid can flow out, otherwise they drown in it – not a particularly nice way to go.

We have two worm farms at home, as we cook often and generate lots of green waste. I have noticed that the worms are much more active in the warmer months, so sometimes in winter our food scraps end up in the compost bins in the James Street Reserve Community Garden (more on that in the next chapter).

INSTANT ORGANIC MATTER

I'm a big fan of adding a few bags of composted cow manure (as well as compost) to a garden, digging it in well during soil preparation or even adding it as a mulch to the soil surface where existing plants are growing. Manure improves soil structure and performance, and also helps the soil to retain moisture. You can buy it by the bag at the hardware store. You could also throw a few big handfuls of pelletized chicken manure on top of the cow. Chook poo is rich in nitrogen, helping the foliage to grow well, so it's great for most fruit and vegies. Be careful though – too much nitrogen can lead to a lush, verdant tomato plant which doesn't actually produce any fruit.

Another good way to improve your soil is to add a few good handfuls of blood and bone, a classic slow-release fertiliser, which will add some trace elements and minerals into the soil. It's a good idea to leave your soil for a few weeks after adding the manures before you start planting.

MULCHING

Mulching involves covering the soil with a layer of organic material, pebbles or even cardboard to help insulate it against extremes. This helps the soil to retain moisture, moderates its temperature, and suppresses weeds, and organic mulch breaks down and fertilises the soil as well. There are many kinds of mulch on the market and the choice can be overwhelming, but, as a rule of thumb, coarse loose mulches provide the highest benefits. Apply mulches no more deeply than 2 to 5 centimetres over the soil. I like to use pea straw or chopped lucerne mulch on my garden, because they add nitrogen to the top layer of soil as they break down. Tea tree and sugar cane products are widely promoted as mulch; they can help reduce moisture loss, although in my experience, they don't really improve the soil. The best mulch is a layer of rich compost from your own heap in the garden.

WATERING

The finger test is the best way to see if your potting mix or soil is dry and needs watering. Stick your finger in – if soil or potting mix stick to your finger, and it feels damp, it probably is. On hot summer days I water my garden daily, at other times, less often – just check the soil, and water if it feels dry. Pots and containers should be checked daily and watered as required, as they are very prone to drying out, especially in windy weather.

It's better to water your garden in the morning rather than at night. Excess water lying around on leaves at night can lead to fungal problems, and also makes it easier for snails and slugs to come creeping round and munch on your booty! Make sure you are actually deep-watering the soil, rather than just doing a superficial job on the top layer and leaves. If you get the water to the roots of the plants, this will encourage them to grow deeper into the soil. If your garden is well-mulched you may not need to water it every day, but it's always best to check – especially in the heat of summer.

SUNLIGHT

Ideally, find some open, sunny space to grow productive plants. If you have all-day sun and face north that's perfect, but as long as your plants get at least four hours of direct sunlight each day that should be enough for them to thrive. A position in the morning sun (which is what my front garden has) should provide enough sunlight for fruit and vegies to grow well.

My vegie garden has deciduous trees overhead, which let through the winter sun, but block the summer sun, so I tend to plant leafy greens such as rocket and lettuce which cope better with the shade. If your garden has a westerly aspect, this can be harsh on delicate salad vegies or tender rhubarb leaves, shading them in the morning and blasting them with sun in the afternoon. You may need to find cooler spots for these if you can.

GROWING EDIBLES IN POTS

If you have no soil or open ground, it's easy to grow edibles in pots, as long as you have enough sunlight. Their light and water requirements are just the same as if they were planted in the ground. One thing to remember is that pots need to be able to drain freely, so raise them slightly, using pieces of rubber, tile or small feet. A big plus of growing edibles in pots is that you can put them on castors, allowing you to move them around to follow the sun, and to take them with you if you move home.

You will need to use a good-quality Premium potting mix – it's important to spend money here and buy the premium product, which has good drainage and also good water retention. Just plant your seedlings directly into pots, making sure you give them enough space to grow. Check the label to see how large the plants

Tomatoes, basil and Vietnamese mint can all be grown in pots.

will grow, and the recommended spacing, so you allow enough space for the plant to grow in all directions. Plants like herbs, lettuce and rocket can be planted in pots 20 to 30 centimetres in diameter, whilst larger plants like rhubarb will need a pot with a diameter of at least 50 centimetres. Use lucerne mulch on top to help the soil retain moisture, and be aware that plants in pots will dry out in hot, windy conditions much more quickly than plants in the ground.

Potting mix doesn't have all of the goodness and nutrients that soil does, so you will need to feed your pots regularly to help the plants along. A worm farm is a perfect hand-in-glove fit for gardening in containers, as the worm wee will provide most of the nutrients required in an organic manner, and it can be diluted with water at a 1:10 rate and applied as liquid food. Failing this, apply a liquid fertiliser according to the instructions. Choose an organic one, such as fish emulsion or seaweed fertiliser, rather than a chemical one. You could also apply pelletised chicken manure to help leafy veg grow, as it adds nitrogen to the potting mix as it breaks down.

There are many pots to choose from to ensure your potted edible garden looks like part of your home, although there is nothing to stop you from using recycled black plastic pots from your friendly local nursery or garden centre, if you ask them nicely!

Adults enjoy harvest time too – especially me, when the rhubarb's going into a pie.

WHAT TO GROW

The plants below represent a tiny slice of what's available today to home gardeners. These are the easy-to-grow vegetables I grow in my own small garden so there's something fresh to harvest all year round. They can all be grown in small spaces or containers.

BEANS

Dwarf French beans are not climbers, but low-growing bushy plants which need no support. Ideal for compact vegie plots, they also grow in containers. Beans are a warm season crop and don't like disturbance, so plant seeds directly where they are to grow. Sow seeds 2.5 centimetres deep in damp soil or potting mix anytime from early spring into summer. Beans need a sunny, well-drained spot and grow best in soil enriched with aged manure prior to planting. Use a good-quality potting mix in containers.

Space seeds 15 centimetres apart to give them room to form a bush about 45 centimetres high. Don't overwater, especially before seeds germinate, as they prefer a drier soil. Dwarf beans take about ten weeks to grow, flower and begin forming pods. Keep picking and expect them to crop for several weeks.

Harvest beans while they are young and tender, so the pods don't become tough and woody, and the plant keeps on producing. Liquid feeding every seven to ten days also helps to keep plants productive. Where space permits, plant a few seeds every four weeks until late summer for a constant supply of beans well into autumn.

BEETROOT

Beetroot is a wonderful vegetable. You can eat its leafy tops in a salad and harvest the round, red root to bake, boil or eat raw. The tops are rich in magnesium so if you don't eat the leaves, make sure they go to the compost bin! Start by digging aged manure into your soil, then sow the seeds directly into the ground in a sunny position. They'll also grow in a pot, but select baby varieties.

Plant seeds from early spring through to summer or early autumn. Sow them into shallow drills 1.2 centimetres deep, then thin out the small seedlings so they are 20 to 30 centimetres apart. Each beetroot seed is actually a seed cluster, so make sure you remove extra seedlings to avoid over-crowding. Beetroot plants need regular watering, and also respond well to a liquid fertiliser with seaweed applied every seven to ten days. Beetroot will be ready to pull from the ground after ten to twelve weeks, sometimes longer.

BROAD BEANS

Sow seeds to grow these striking plants in autumn or winter, so they're ready for picking in mid to late spring and into early summer. There are two forms of broad beans: dwarf and tall. In a small space or a container, go for dwarf broad beans unless you have a sunny vertical wall to support the tall climbing form. Plant seeds 20 centimetres apart and stagger the rows in a bed, or just pop a few seedlings into a large container. To support the plants – even the dwarf varieties – use timber stakes and string around the circumference of the planting. Climbing forms can reach 2 metres or more, so they need tall stakes or a trellis.

Whens the beans are flowering, pinch out new top growth to give the plants extra energy to direct into fruiting. Pick the beans while they are small to eat steamed and whole, or wait until the pods are large and swollen and eat the bean inside the pod. Once they have finished cropping, dig the plants into the soil or toss them into the compost and allow them to break down.

BROCCOLI

There are many different kinds of broccoli but I grow two: the common green variety and the more unusual vivid, purple sprouting broccoli. There is also the popular broccolini, which is grown in the same way as broccoli. All are pretty straightforward to grow in the ground or in a container. Broccoli needs a compost-enriched soil and at least six hours of sunlight each day. Sow seeds or plant seedlings in spring, summer and early autumn, but note that plants grow best through the cooler months of the year. Space the seeds or seedlings about 40 centimetres apart and expect them to grow up to 60 centimetres high.

Harvest the delicious green heads about ten weeks after planting, while the buds are tightly closed. Once the main head has been harvested, keep picking the smaller side shoots and leaves. Plants can be productive for up to six months, so keep them strong with regular watering and fortnightly liquid feeding.

CARROTS

Carrots are probably the second most popular homegrown vegetable, after tomatoes. They are easy to grow – just make sure you have an open, free-draining, stone-free soil in a sunny position. To create a good soil for the roots to grow in, dig the soil well to at least a spade's depth. Don't add manure before planting as this may encourage 'forking', or deformed roots. Plant seeds in autumn or spring in shallow rows about 0.6 centimetres deep. Cover seeds lightly with soil, pressing them firmly into the soil, keep moist and wait for them to sprout in around ten to twenty days. Thin out seedlings to about 5 centimetres apart to give those left space to grow.

Apply a liquid feed fortnightly and expect to start harvesting your own homegrown carrots in about eighteen weeks (about ten to twelve weeks for baby carrots). To grow carrots successfully in a container, select baby carrot varieties with short roots. Carrots are great to grow with kids. Encouraging them to pull the carrots straight out of the ground is a good way to get them to eat more vegies.

CELERY

You can't make a good broth without celery! (You also need carrot and onion, the perfect trifecta.) I always use it when I am making stock with the carcass of a roast chicken and, for that reason, it's handy to have celery growing. It's pretty trouble-free, but this is a plant that loves lots of water. I have also found that a fortnightly feed of organic liquid fertiliser prevents it from becoming stringy and tough.

Some people like to wrap the plants in brown paper to blanch the stems and keep them mellow in flavour, but I don't bother as I like the strong flavour in my broths. I do, however, mulch around the stems with straw to keep the roots from drying out.

Start seeds in winter or early spring in punnets then plant seedlings out in spring or early summer when the little plants are big enough to handle. Celery grows best in soil that's been well-prepared with manure and a dash of lime, and can also be planted in a container, using a good-quality potting mix. Space plants about 30 to 40 centimetres apart, or plant one into a pot 25 to 30 centimetres in diameter. With regular, thorough watering and fortnightly liquid feeding you can harvest celery after about twenty weeks.

CHILLI

These productive little plants provide good colour in the vegie patch as well as a little fire in your cooking. With many chillies, the smaller the fruit, the hotter the spice factor. There are chillies with a milder taste, or you may prefer to grow the large fruited capsicums, which are sweet rather than hot. Chillies like warm growing conditions, so sow seeds about 0.6 centimetres deep in punnets during spring through to early summer. When planting out seedlings into the garden, space them at least 50 to 60 centimetres apart, or allocate one plant to a large container.

Keep chilli plants well-watered and regularly fed with a liquid plant fertiliser applied every two weeks. They should produce fruit about three months after planting. Chillies keep producing through summer and autumn, and, in many areas, can be kept growing through winter.

CUCUMBER

Cucumbers are very rewarding to grow over spring and summer, either in a garden or in a large container. In a garden, choose a sunny spot with good soil and plant seeds or seedlings directly where they are to grow. In a container or small space, train them up a tripod or several stakes, and look for patio varieties, which grow to a compact 90 to 150 centimetres. In a garden, space plants at least 50 centimetres apart, and just grow one plant to a large container.

Plant in spring through to summer in most areas but in warm, frost-free areas they grow through most of the year. Cucumbers grow quickly and can start producing fruit within ten to fourteen weeks of planting. Encourage strong growth with daily watering and by liquid feeding vines every two weeks. Vines generally produce for many weeks, but if you want cucumbers throughout summer, make successive plantings every four to six weeks.

GARLIC

To grow your own garlic, plant cloves in autumn or early winter (give them protection from frost in cold zones). You can grow garlic from the bulbs in your kitchen, but for best results buy a head of organic garlic. Separate the cloves and plant them into a free-draining soil 2 centimetres deep and 10 to 15 centimetres apart in a sunny spot. Alternatively, pop a couple of cloves into a container. Use only firm, dry cloves with their skins on.

They grow slowly for about five months, and are ready once their leaves begin to yellow, after the plants have flowered – usually in late spring or early summer. If you don't want the plants to flower, harvest the buds and toss them into a salad. Garlic needs to grow strongly to form good-sized cloves, so keep the plants well-watered. In spring feed once a week with a liquid plant food. As the plants mature, reduce feeding to once a month. Harvest the entire plant, keeping the bulbs and stems intact, and leave them in the sun for a few days before storing them in a cool, dry, airy place.

KALE

This easy-to-grow plant is great if you have only limited space as it is very attractive and it keeps on giving. Leaves can be ready to harvest just seven weeks from planting. There many varieties, but my favourite is Tuscan Black, also known as cavolo nero, which has long, green-black leaves. Kale is quite forgiving, but grows best in firm, compost-enriched soil, with reliable moisture. Plants can also be grown in containers – use one plant per container.

Kale is usually grown as a winter and spring crop, but it grows year round in cooler areas. Sow seeds in mid-summer to autumn, and plant out seedlings in autumn. Space the seedlings of large varieties such as Tuscan Black 40 to 50 centimetres apart. Applying a liquid fertiliser with seaweed every two weeks helps to produce lovely, healthy plants.

LETTUCE

I like the more robust Cos lettuce, as well as bitter, red-leafed radicchio (which is actually a type of chicory). Lettuces grow year round but are best grown through spring and summer. You can harvest them about eight to ten weeks from planting. To maintain a constant crop, keep planting a few seeds every few weeks in a seed tray. Sow seeds about 0.3 centimetres deep, and cover them lightly. Plant seedlings into troughs or rows in a vegetable patch about 20 to 30 centimetres apart.

They can also be planted among other edibles, such as carrots, strawberries and radish. Don't allow lettuce plants to dry out (water them each day and in summer a little afternoon shade helps) and to keep them growing strongly give them a weekly liquid feed. Oh, and watch out for slugs!

PEAS

Peas are also great to grow with kids – especially the fast-growing snow peas. Kids love picking the pods from the vine and eating them there and then. Peas grow from autumn through to spring. They need support, so use bamboo canes and horizontal string or wire netting. To grow peas in a small space, plant several into a large tub and train them up a tripod of stakes. Sow the seeds where they are to grow, and about 10 centimetres apart in row or near their support.

The seeds germinate best in moist soil, so water them in well but then don't water until the first signs of germination. The peas will appear after they flower. Pick while they are still small and tender as this will encourage the other pods to develop. I often just end up picking them and eating them straight off the vine – I'm too impatient to cook them!

POTATO

Spuds need a sunny, open spot that's been prepared by digging in some compost or aged manure. Plant them in late winter or spring, and give them lots of water. You can sprout any organic potato, but certified seed potatoes are the best as they are virus-free. To get the spud to sprout, place it somewhere bright but out of direct sun. You can plant the whole potato or cut a larger potato into several sprouted pieces.

Once the sprouts are several centimetres long, plant the potato or pieces into a shallow trench in the vegie patch, a raised garden bed or into a large container, such as a 40-litre pot. Cover lightly, building up soil or potting mix around the shoots as the plants grow. If you are planting a few, plant them about 20 centimetres apart.

To keep them growing vigorously, liquid feed them every few weeks, and then apply some pelletised chicken manure after about eight weeks. Keep the roots well covered with soil and mulch. Potatoes need to grow for three to four months before they are ready to harvest, so wait until the plants have flowered and begun to die back before carefully lifting the potatoes out with a fork. I always think that harvesting potatoes is one of the most rewarding gardening experiences – especially if you are doing it with young ones.

RADISH

Ah radishes! Fond memories of the first thing I ever planted with my dad. To keep them growing quickly, add fertiliser or manure to the soil prior to planting and liquid feed weekly as the plants grow. Plant them in spring to autumn, sowing the seeds directly into sunny ground about 0.6 centimetres deep and cover lightly with soil or potting mix. Radishes are easy and quick to grow (they take about four weeks from planting to harvest) virtually all year round.

Grow them among other vegies, in a row or in troughs where space is limited. Radishes should be thinned out as they grow so they are about 3 to 5 centimetres apart. There are a few different varieties, including the large white daikon radish and some tiny varieties that are excellent for growing in containers.

RHUBARB

I'm so proud of my rhubarb and it asks very little of me. I eat it all the time with Bircher muesli, in a crumble or just with a massive spoon of ice-cream. Stew the stems on a low heat with lots of orange rind, a small knob of finely cut ginger and two tablespoons of honey – heaven!

The keys to success are good, rich soil and reliable moisture, along with protection from hot winds and the hot western sun. Rhubarb is a perennial grown from a root, known as a crown. Plant crowns in winter or early spring. Rhubarb needs to be planted so the crown sits just above the soil level. Set plants 50 to 80 centimetres apart, as they form a huge clump over time. Feed regularly with aged cow or chicken manure, or blood and bone.

Harvest them when the stems are about as thick as your thumb, which can be several months from when the shoots erupt in spring. Divide crowns in winter every four to five years with a sharp spade. Most people prefer red rhubarb but the green stems are just as tasty. For a red stem, look for a red variety. Make sure you don't eat the leaves – these should be discarded into the compost. Rhubarb is a fine-looking and rewarding plant in any vegie patch, and I urge you to give it a go!

ROCKET

This is a firm favourite of mine and also easy to grow. It grows readily from seed, so just scatter seeds where you want plants to grow. Lightly cover them with soil or potting mix. Just sow a few seeds at a time to keep a constant supply growing for much of the year. You can start picking leaves a few weeks after sowing. Rocket needs a sunny spot, but do protect it from the hot summer afternoon sun so it doesn't come under too much stress.

Although rocket grows easily, don't neglect it altogether. Water it frequently and apply liquid fertiliser every seven to ten days to keep it powering along. Once these plants flower, their leaves become very peppery in flavour and you may want to remove them to make way for fresh plants. However, if you leave some to flower and seed, you'll have rocket seedlings popping up everywhere – even in paving cracks – so you'll never be without it.

SORREL

Some people think of sorrel as a weed, but I think this culinary herb with its lemon-flavoured leaves adds interest in salads, sauces or even soups. It is very versatile – it will grow in sun or shade, and even produces leaves in winter when you may be short of greens in the vegie garden. This is a deep-rooted plant so it is at its best in good, deep soil that's had plenty of aged manure compost worked in before planting.

If you are growing it in a container, grow one plant per pot and use good-quality potting mix which holds moisture. You'll need to grow sorrel from seed, and the seeds can be planted at any time, but it is best sown in autumn or winter for a late winter to spring harvest. Plants grow to around 45 centimetres high and should be spaced about 20 to 30 centimetres apart. Liquid feed to encourage strong leaf growth and regularly remove flower stems to keep the plant leafy.

SPRING ONION

Sow seeds of these easy-to-grow plants any time, but they grow well from spring into summer planted directly where they are to grow. Choose a sunny spot with well-drained soil or grow them in containers. Make a shallow row about 0.6 centimetres deep, and space seeds about 0.5 centimetres apart. Lightly cover the seeds, then keep the area moist (but not wet) while seeds germinate. To keep the crop coming, keep planting every two weeks. Spring onions grow quickly and you can harvest them eight to ten weeks after you sow them.

STRAWBERRY

Strawbs are very easy and satisfying to grow at home, and are also very child-friendly. Plant them in late winter or early spring, They like full sun and a rich, moisture-retentive soil, so, ideally, dig in composted manure a few weeks before you plant. Strawberries are quite thirsty, so keep plants well-watered, especially when they are flowering and forming fruit in early spring, when you should also apply a liquid fertiliser with seaweed every eight to ten days. Some varieties keep producing crops into summer – whenever you see them flowering, give them a hit of liquid fertiliser.

After fruiting, strawberries send out lots of runners (long side shoots). These form new plants, but are best removed, and can be used to grow new plants. Strawberry plants tend to fruit well for two to three years, then it's best to replace them by planting the developing plants from each runner or buying new plants. Once the new ones are established and have taken root, you can remove the parent plant. Use lucerne or straw mulch to keep fruit off the ground and free of rot and pests.

TOMATO

Everyone loves picking a tomato from a vine – and absolutely nothing beats the smell and taste of a homegrown one! Use seedlings and, if you haven't grown them before, start with cherry tomatoes, which are very forgiving and produce lots of fruit. Plant them in late spring to summer or all year round in warm, frost-free areas.

Tomatoes need a warm, sheltered, sunny environment and good air circulation. Support them with a stake at least 2 metres high. As they grow, tie the stem to the stake using soft ties.

If the vine starts to get too bushy, nip out the laterals (the small shoots which grow from the main stem, forming side branches). This also encourages the vine to put its energy into fruiting. Don't be afraid to pinch out the top shoot if the vine grows higher than its stake. Water daily, and feed every seven to fourteen days with a liquid tomato fertiliser. Tomatoes usually take at least twelve weeks from planting to harvest, and continue fruiting for many weeks. Unfortunately, tomatoes attract lots of pests, so use a tomato dust regularly and, in fruit fly zones, use something to control them or your crop will be ruined. There are environmentally-friendly pest and fruit fly control measures for tomatoes.

FURTHER READING

What I have given you here is really just an introduction to enable you to start growing your own food. It certainly is a journey of discovery and there is so much detailed knowledge on growing particular kinds of crops and wonderful experience out there. I urge you to just have a go.

There are some wonderful books, more detailed than this, that will help you to develop your growing skills. Have a look at Jamie Durie's *Edible Garden Design* (Penguin, 2013), and if you live in an apartment, Indira Naidoo's book, *The Edible Balcony* (Penguin, 2011) is a ripper, full of detailed growing tips as well as wonderful recipes. I also suggest you look at *The Organic Guide to Edible Gardens* by Jennifer Stackhouse and Debbie McDonald (Murdoch Books, 2012) and Meredith Kirton's *Harvest: A Complete Australian Guide to the Edible Garden* (Murdoch Books, 2009). *The Yates Garden Guide* is also invaluable.

I subscribe to the *Organic Gardener*, published bi-monthly by the ABC, and am an avid viewer of the weekly *Gardening Australia* on the ABC, which regularly champions the benefits of homegrown produce.

WHAT TO PLANT WHEN

SPRING PLANTING

beans	corn	rhubarb
capsicum	leek	rocket
carrot	lettuce	sorrel
celery	potato	strawberry
chilli	radish	tomato

SUMMER PLANTING

beans	chilli	rocket
capsicum	corn	spring onion
carrot	lettuce	tomato
celery	okra	

AUTUMN PLANTING

beetroot	cauliflower	onion
broad beans	celery	peas
broccoli	kale	radish
Brussels sprouts	leek	rhubarb
cabbage	lettuce	rocket
carrot	mustard	

WINTER PLANTING

beetroot	kale	potato
broad beans	leek	radish
carrot	lettuce	rhubarb
cauliflower	mustard	rocket
celery	onion	
garlic	peas	

ESSENTIAL HERBS

basil	oregano	tarragon
chives	parsley	thyme
coriander	rosemary	Vietnamese mint
mint	sage	

Organic Producers

Up until now I have been talking about growing your own edibles at home, but I thought I might introduce you to a couple of producers who are growing and distributing edibles on a large scale – Lesley and Quentin Bland, from Kurrawong Organics, and Marty Boetz, from the Cook's Co-op. I think what they are doing is pretty inspiring. If we understood the labour and love that goes into commercial food-growing, we might waste less of it.

KURRAWONG ORGANIC FARM

Nestled somewhere between Bathurst and Lithgow is the amazing Kurrawong Organic Farm. I first met its owners, Lesley and Quentin, at Eveleigh Farmers' Market in Sydney's Darlington, where they sell their produce every Saturday. They grow the best brassicas (the family name for cauliflowers, Brussels sprouts, cabbages, kales and broccoli, among other things) I have ever tasted.

I love the history surrounding the family and their property, as it gives such an interesting insight into early rural life. Quentin grew up on the hundred-acre property, and his family has farmed there for four generations, including his and Lesley's sons, Harry, Alexander and Tobias. In 1931 Quentin's grandfather, Charles Bland, delivered the first Brussels sprouts grown in New South Wales to the old Haymarket for sale.

When Quentin took over the farm it consisted mainly of apple and pear orchards, along with some Brussels sprouts, cabbages and cauliflowers. At the time, the government was offering financial incentives to encourage farmers to replace orchards with other crops, so Quentin removed most of the orchards to make way for market garden crops. Broccoli became popular in the '70s, and he started to grow it in a serious way. Today he plants over a million broccoli seedlings each year.

The farm has always been run on organic principles. 'Managing the soil is really important – we need to farm it, not mine it,' says Quentin. 'We have been farming this soil for over ninety years and it's still just as rich as it was back when we started.' At Kurrawong they leave the land fallow for two years following one year of planting. This three-year crop rotation scheme has played a key role in the farm's success, allowing the soil to rest and recuperate. When he plants again, Quentin uses a different group of plants to help reduce pests and soil-borne diseases.

This explains why we pay more for sustainably farmed produce, and why it's worth paying the extra – the land lies empty for two years, recovering and re-energising after putting all its goodness into growing gorgeous vegies. We need more farmers like these guys, who care for the environment as well as the produce they grow.

Most of the farm's produce is sent to distributors in Sydney, before being sold into supermarkets and other chains all around Australia. Growing broccoli on this scale is a serious business, which makes this nutritious crop available to a large number of people. I think it's such a noble thing to be growing and supplying good, nutritious food like this.

However, once the produce leaves their farm, Quentin and Lesley have no control over how long it takes to reach the consumer's table. To my mind, the real magic happens when they bring their produce into the city themselves. They started by selling directly to a couple of select retailers in Sydney, ensuring that the food was in the store only a day or two after harvesting.

OPPOSITE With Lesley Bland from Kurrawong Organics, handling the precious Brussels sprouts.

TOP Fields of goodness – after this crop the land will remain fallow for two years so the soil can recover.

BOTTOM Jerusalem artichokes.

Eveleigh Farmers' Market in Sydney, a wonderful way to buy produce in the inner-city.

'We had a basic herb and vegetable garden at home which we enjoyed growing for ourselves, and if we had extra we would sell it into Wholefoods House in town,' explains Lesley.

They started selling at Eveleigh Farmers' Market about four years ago. Lesley says, 'It was a perfect opportunity for more people to be able to buy our product, and, as demand grew, we expanded and planted more and more different lines.' The food they sell at the market is harvested and picked on Thursday, then goes straight into refrigeration, before being transported to Sydney on Friday and sold on Saturday.

They also now sell at Sydney Sustainable Markets in Taylor Square, Darlinghurst. Taking their food to market is very much Lesley's passion; she loves the interaction with people and the relationships that have developed from the face-to-face contact with people coming to buy their gorgeous fresh fruit and veg. There is indeed something very comforting and real in this 'old school' relationship between farmer and consumer. The food is not in a massive, faceless fridge all wrapped in plastic, with no sign of where it has come from. Instead, it is as fresh as it can be, and you can see that it's bursting with goodness straight from the vibrant, rich earth it came from, rather than coming from some hydroponic greenhouse.

Lesley tells me, 'I take pride in taking down a quality product, something I have grown, nurtured and harvested myself, and seeing people react to it at the market; it's magic.'

Life is never quiet on the farm; there is work to be done all year round, with the constant cycle of planting and harvesting. Lesley and Quentin plant their brassicas from early spring; at the time of writing, in October, they had already planted 100 000 broccoli, which will be ready to harvest at Christmas. Subsequent plantings occur weekly from October through to March, ensuring there is a regular supply to harvest each week up until the beginning of August.

Quentin and Lesley now plant their other plants every fortnight to ensure there is a constant supply for the markets. When they started off at Eveleigh they sold seven vegetables; today they sell over thirty, including kale, silverbeet, spinach, beetroot, fennel, lettuce, tomatoes, cucumber, rocket, rhubarb, zucchini, squash, corn, and potatoes.

Quentin and Lesley also support other farmers in their region by selling their produce at the Eveleigh stall. In turn, the farmers in Orange sell Kurrawong's produce further out west. This simple relationship between the farmers enables their produce to be made available to yet more people.

What I love, is that by working in the farmers' markets themselves, farmers have direct contact with their customers, so can develop a personal relationship with them. It could be a discussion on how the produce was cooked the previous week, an exchange of ideas, tips and recipes, or feedback on what they grow. The farmers learn what their own food tastes like and this completes the cycle of growing and farming. How satisfying that must be to a grower.

Each time I cook Kurrawong Brussels sprouts, kale or any of their produce, I absolutely savour them. I respect the work and energy, of both the soil and the human hand, that has gone into their creation. Okay – this may sound too New Age for some, but for me, each time I eat their food it is akin to having a spiritual experience. It's the same feeling I get when I eat something from my own garden, or from the community garden. I have great respect for the food and for the fact that it sustains me and others I love when I cook for them.

MARTIN BOETZ'S COOKS CO-OP

There has never been a time when we've shown such an interest in fresh, healthy produce, and now many restaurants, including Matt Moran's Chiswick and the Grounds of Alexandria, are getting in on the act, with their own kitchen gardens. For restaurants that don't have the space for an on-site garden, this is a great alternative.

Marty Boetz, co-creator of Longrain restaurants in Sydney and Melbourne, and executive chef at Rushcutters in Sydney, has embarked on an ambitious and exciting farming project in Sackville in the Hawkesbury region.

For as long as I have known him, Marty has been passionate about sourcing and using good-quality produce. Meat always had to be pasture-fed and free range. Fruit and veg had to be the freshest available. A few years ago, he decided to take this love of top-quality seasonal produce one step further by growing food on his own land. He bought an old turf farm on 28 acres of fertile land on the banks of the Hawkesbury River, and started to plough the fields, cultivate the soil and begin planting a fruit and market garden on part of that land. He now has complete control over what he grows and how he grows it, as well as ensuring that what he uses in his food is the freshest available – picked that day, or the day before.

Now he is planning to encourage other chefs and restaurateurs to grow their own food on a plot at his farm – to join his Cooks Co-op, so they can share stories, skills and connect with each other whilst growing the food that they want to cook with. Marty has also converted one of the barns on the property into a drive-in coolroom, allowing him to act as a distributor for other local farmers in the Hawkesbury region as well. This relationship gives these small, independent growers a wider network and access to the city restaurant scene, strengthening their businesses and helping to keep their farms viable. Marty sells a selection of their local produce, ranging from honey, to prawns, to free-range pork.

Today he delivers his food into some of Sydney's leading restaurants, and this direct relationship means that if they don't choose to grow their own at his farm, he can grow it for them, or source exactly what they want from local producers. At a time when the farming of our food is becoming more and more industrialised by large conglomerates, it's important to support small, local, independent producers by finding markets for them and thus making their produce available for us to enjoy.

OPPOSITE PAGE Marty has always been passionate about good-quality produce – now he grows it himself.

ABOVE Fresh fennel.

LEFT Marty and I at the farm.

CHAPTER 4

Share

In an ideal world, everyone would grow their own fruit and vegies, or at least some of them, at home. But that's just not an option for some people, whether because of lack of space, lack of time, or just lack of know-how. If this is you, I urge you to think about a great alternative, which is growing enormously in popularity – the community garden. Speaking from my own experience with the James Street Reserve Community Garden, just behind my shop, I can't recommend community gardening more highly. Not only do you get to participate in the joys of growing your own food, but you connect with your community at the same time.

There is great significance in the connection between like-minded people who grow food – between grower and customer, or just between neighbours, friends and loved ones who enjoy growing, cooking and eating food together. It's all part of the holistic bigger picture of feeling connected and feeling 'part of' rather than 'apart from'.

James Street Reserve Community Garden, Redfern

GETTING STARTED

I am incredibly lucky to have been involved in this fantastic project almost from the word go. Back in 2009, a few of the locals on the western side of Young Street came together with a plan to beautify the laneway at the back of their terraces. They painted old pots bright pink and filled old laundry sinks with succulents. There were all kinds of other urban creativity, and the laneway was gradually transformed. As an extension of the greening of the laneway, the idea of creating a community garden started to grow in the collective consciousness of a core group.

I was approached by Tam, who lives on Young Street, to see if I was interested in supporting the James Street Reserve Community Garden (JSRCG) project. The plan was to build the garden in part of a small park, St James Reserve, located in the back lane behind my store. It was a sad little space, with just a couple of benches facing a huge graffiti wall; it lacked spirit and was often inhabited by some of the destitute, troubled folk who lived in the area. It wasn't a place where you would want to hang out and kick a ball with your kids, and you certainly wouldn't wander through there at night.

I loved the fact that this group of locals had been eyeing off this derelict, decrepit park and had this vision to create a vibrant garden for everyone, and I didn't have to think twice about joining them. I had just returned from a trip to New York, where I had noticed how the little pockets of community gardens throughout Manhattan really energised their surroundings, making such a difference to the local area. The aim of the JSRCG group was to make the garden into a 'safe space that welcomes everyone, encourages community spirit, facilitates learning and information exchange and acts as a sustainability role model'. What's not to love about that?

As it turned out, the group planning the garden was very switched-on and highly organised. There were people from a whole range of backgrounds – everything from project management and marketing to landscape architecture. At the time I joined, the committee had been meeting, discussing and planning the project for some months and was in the throes of preparing a submission to the City of Sydney

OPPOSITE Our poor scarecrow was stolen once, then reappeared mysteriously about four months later. That's my shirt and waistcoat by the way – he's a very dapper chap!

ABOVE With the always colourful Yvonne, and a crop of celeriac.

BELOW Sunflowers brighten up the garden.

Council. To secure some much-needed funding, we applied for a grant under the Council's matching grant scheme, where they matched cash contributions and volunteer time, up to a maximum of $10 000. We also needed Council approval to build on the land, which was part of a public park.

As the first official 'President', Janet was a major cog in the wheel of getting the garden off the ground, overseeing all communications with the Council and making sure we ticked all the right boxes. It was a huge task. A project manager by profession, she volunteered to pull the grant together, with other group members providing information on budget, design layout and how the garden would be run. We worked out initial construction costs, including the cost of people's time, as we needed the Council to match this with cash to help pay for fencing, soil, fertiliser and other materials.

We designed six large circular, raised corrugated iron beds to occupy half of the public space. We opted for circular beds to maximise the available space and raised beds because we had concerns over soil quality, with possible contamination by previous use. By using raised beds with a filter layer underneath we could minimise any problems, and also control the soil and drainage. We fenced the garden off to provide some security, but decided on an open-gate policy to anyone who wanted to come in and experience the space.

It took us nearly twelve months to obtain Council funding and approval. This was the first time anyone had tried to create a community garden on Council land within a public park, so the Council had no precedent (it now has a Community Gardens Policy, located on its website at www.cityofsydney.nsw.gov.au). I should say that, although the process seemed to take a long time, the Council was very supportive from day one. Today, they call us the trailblazers, and hold us up as an example of what a community can achieve.

UP AND RUNNING

Once we had the green light, we swung into action, putting the beds together and filling them with soil before we finally started planting and developing our thriving little patch of goodness right in the heart of Redfern. We agreed to use organic gardening principles, with no pesticides, and that we would all share equally in the harvest.

ABOVE Chives look good, taste good and repel insects as well.

RIGHT Garden plan of the James Street Reserve Community Garden.

OPPOSITE Working bees are always hives of activity as well as a great way to catch up with what's been going on with other members.

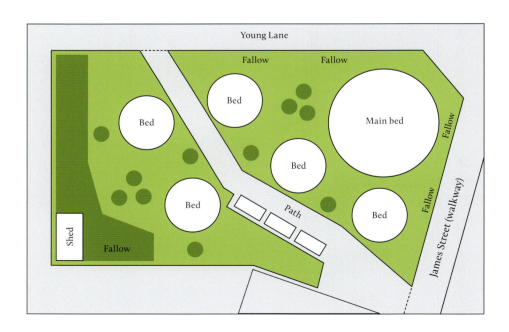

We came up with a garden plan based on communal garden beds, each run by its own team, which was responsible for crop selection, planting and maintenance of that bed. We decided to rotate the crops on a seasonal basis to keep the soil healthy, and we planted out the fallow areas between the beds with mixed annuals, herbs and other plants, including rhubarb, potatoes, mint and thyme. These fallow areas act as an attractant to insects, so they munch on these and not on our crops. We also planted a row of citrus, quince and nut trees down one side of the garden.

The Mayor of Sydney, Clover Moore, opened the garden on 30 October 2010, and since then we have gone from strength to strength, producing bananas, kiwi fruit, strawberries, potatoes, sweet potatoes, pumpkin (in a no-dig garden), parsnips, barley, radishes and broad beans, nearly all the herbs you can think of, mustard greens, collards, and a few unusual plants, such as warrigal greens and amaranth. We now have our own compost area and thriving worm farm as well, fed by food scraps from local residents and businesses. Our funding comes from annual membership fees of $20, plus donations of cash and materials from some community-minded local businesses (including ours!).

We decided we needed a garden shed, and it was my baby to design and build. We have just finished building it in the corner of the garden. It is made from reclaimed materials, and (subject to neighbourhood approval) we hope to have a native bee hive sitting on top of the shed in the coming months – how cool is that?

On the first Saturday of each month members get together for a working bee. It's a great opportunity to discuss the plans for the garden, shovel some manure off a ute and just congregate and be part of the community. Our members comprise a cross-section of locals, including families, couples with dogs, oldies and youngsters, and our working bees are lively affairs. Twig café, which operates from part of the Garden Life premises, brings us morning tea halfway through; how very civilised!

Since the garden has been installed, the use of the park has changed massively. I often see local residents and workers enjoying lunch breaks in the space; just recently, when we were building the shed, I saw a grandmother pointing out different crops to her grandchildren. The garden is a great resource not only for members, but for all those who walk past, helping them to understand where food comes from and how it's grown.

We have a few smaller beds in concrete pipes that we encourage non-members and locals to pick from, to try to reduce our losses. We have lost a few things along the way, often just as they are reaching their prime (a prize pumpkin was once ripped out), but there has been no massive vandalism, and, the way I see it, the occasional loss is all part of the bigger picture of having a thriving produce garden in the middle of the city. The garden is a constant source of joy and learning for me and everyone else involved.

I like to think that we are using the garden as a tool for further education, inspiring others to grow their own or to go one step further and set up a community garden. We hold regular workshops, including special kids' workshops, and conduct tours for other interested community groups. Check out our blog at www.jsrcg.blogspot.com.au – you will find some inspiring news and images from our working bees. If you are in the area, make sure you come to see us and say 'Hi!'.

OPPOSITE TOP Short bamboo canes protect young, tender foliage.

OPPOSITE BOTTOM LEFT Richard Francis, the chef from Twig café, tends his plot.

OPPOSITE BOTTOM RIGHT Young zucchini and flower.

BELLOW Jon is a never ending source of wisdom and inspiration in the garden

BOTTOM parsley seeds ready to harvest

Some of the Locals

JANET (THE YOUNGER)

Although the garden is definitely a group effort, Janet was the driving force who really made it happen. A few years back, Janet and her husband Mick moved into Young Street. Working from home and caring for her new son, Will, Janet felt disconnected from other locals, so, her first Christmas there, she decided to organise a street get-together – about forty people showed up, and it was a huge success.

Like everyone else, Janet hated the park at the back of her house. One day, at her mothers' group, people started to discuss community gardens, and there was a strong desire to teach their youngsters where fresh food and veg come from. The park was the obvious place.

Janet rounded up some other residents, and quickly took charge of the community garden project. Now that the garden is flourishing, Janet shines when she talks about it, especially the impact it has had on her son's behaviour and habits. She told me, 'The kids come to working bees, they are part of the community, they know all our neighbours, everyone knows them, and they have a sense of belonging which is wider than the family unit . . . as a parent, getting kids to eat vegetables is traumatic, and now they are living in a space where it's all growing all around them.'

The Christmas drinks tradition that Janet started has continued, although now, largely due to her energy and drive, we have a verdant, productive oasis where everyone can come together and celebrate.

JON

Jon has lived in the Redfern area for twelve years, and has a thriving garden business, working all over Sydney. We are very lucky to have him, as he has the most amazing knowledge of permaculture and organic gardening practices. He is the 'go to' person for advice, directs every working bee, and is largely responsible for the garden's vibrancy and success.

The word 'community' evokes a feeling of belonging for Jon. He told me, 'Before this garden started, I would have been hard-pressed to name any of my neighbours. Now, I might not know all the names of people who pass the garden, but they all nod, say 'hi' and have a chat, and I think people really like that.'

Jon finds that spending time in the garden is a great way to wind down after a day's gardening for clients, but his commitment to the garden is so much greater than his self-interest. He holds training sessions for new members and he gives a lesson at every working bee on some aspect of the garden, whether it's how to build a no-dig garden for our pumpkins, or how to build an arbour from irrigation piping for our climbing beans.

Jon says, 'I really enjoy having the garden here, and I know that if people don't know what they are doing, then it won't last. If it doesn't succeed the land returns to the Council, and I don't want to do that.'

Jon has big plans for the garden; one involves extending the little patch of goodness into the rest of the park to create an orchard, and the other is to build a large arbour structure over the seats, providing shade in summer and a great place to grow vines like passionfruit and pumpkins.

JANET (THE ELDER)

Thank God for Janet, who has lived in Young Street for twenty-three years. Born in 1926, Janet hails from Barellan, a small country town, and was raised on a farm. Her mother was a keen gardener, and her family grew or produced almost everything they ate.

Janet came to Sydney, took her vows in the Catholic Church, and began a life devoted to the service of others. For more than thirty years she taught kids all over Sydney, then, as she approached her middle years, she left her habit behind and began working with the disadvantaged within urban Sydney.

I can't remember the first time I met her, but I gradually became aware of a gentle, elderly woman who would come into the Twig café a couple of times a week for a coffee. We started saying hello, then our chats became longer and quite soon every time I saw her at Twig I wanted to sit down and spend time with her. She told me that the community garden has given her a wonderful opportunity to meet younger people, whom she wouldn't ordinarily meet.

It is through opening my store in such a vibrant area, and also getting involved with the garden, that I've been able to meet special people like Janet whom I ordinarily wouldn't have come into contact with. Connecting with older people like Janet, going round to her house for a cup of tea and a chat, warms my heart and also helps my sense of belonging. To me, Janet truly embodies the spirit of community, with her optimistic spirit, warmth, energy and gentle personality. Among the many things that I love about her is the fact that she is a MASSIVE fan of the Sydney Swans, and has followed them for about forty-five years, until recently attending every match.

SACHA AND LYDIA

Sacha and his partner Lydia (that's her in the green top on page 161) have lived on Little Young Street for the past seven years with their two children, Arkie and Ren, who are always out and about on their bikes in the 'hood.

Sacha is a landscape architect and I remember him declaring adamantly at one of our early committee meetings that the community garden would change social behaviour. I must admit, at the time I thought his statement a bit over-the-top but, as it turns out, he was absolutely right.

Less than thirty metres from the community garden is a humble terrace house, which provides short-term refuge for people who are homeless and struggling with life. Lydia told me that one day, as she was watering the community garden, she had a conversation with a woman staying there. She says, 'We wouldn't ordinarily have felt comfortable with each other. I feel we connected in a way which ordinarily wouldn't have happened, if we weren't in the garden'. We have now approached the refuge to encourage residents to come and help out in the garden, and to join our monthly working bees.

Sacha firmly believes that the garden is a conduit for improved connection between people from all walks of life, telling me, 'For me, the social sustainability side of things is as important, if not more so, than the environmentally sustainable aspects of the garden . . . People will now stop and interact with each other . . . The most beautiful thing about the garden is that it's community-building right before our very eyes.'

Lydia is currently harvesting a bumper crop of coriander, parsley, radishes, broad beans and zebra beans from the bed she works on. 'Jon has really inspired me to have a good go at it', she says of our esteemed guru and head gardener.

Spring Lunch

One of the best things about the community garden is that each year we hold a couple of social events there – usually Christmas drinks and something else. A little while ago we held a spring lunch one Saturday. We wanted to celebrate the new season and our community with a get-together in our little spot of goodness and to taste some of the fruits of our labour. It was a beautiful sunny day, and we sat at three tables along one side of the garden benches, and used bales of lucerne for seats on the other side. We decorated the tables with freshly picked cornflowers and nasturtiums.

I wanted to use as much of our own homegrown produce as possible, so I started by making a rustic pesto with our wonderful warrigal greens, which seem to be on everyone's menu at the moment (make sure you blanch them before you cook with them). They grow really well in the semi-shade of our garden. I put some in a mortar and pestle with some of our basil and parsley and ground it with fresh garlic, almonds (not ours!) and parmesan. I also made a frittata with local Berrima Ridge eggs and cavolo nero from the garden.

Jon had grown some purple, waxy Kipfler potatoes, and Kati had a small harvest of Dutch Creams – it was definitely a case of potato quality over quantity! I parboiled them, then picked some radishes and Dutch carrots, which I combined with a bitey garlic aioli and the pesto to create a garden tasting plate for entree. Okay, so I cheated with the main course; the ocean trout wasn't raised in our garden, nor was the Thirlmere chicken, which I poached, mixed with some mayonnaise and combined with a bunch of our mustard greens.

For dessert, I had my eye on some of our thick-stemmed garden rhubarb. I'm a big fan of the 'barb, dating back to my childhood days, and I stewed some with a little sugar and added some orange zest. Richard from Twig made some delicious chewy meringues and, with some whipped cream, it was HEAVEN!!

It was great just to sit in the space and relax, to share food and stories, and to see everyone sitting together at the one table. My involvement with the garden has taught me so much about the importance of connecting with others in the local community, and the experience has really enriched my daily life. It's remarkable to think of how the run-down park looked before we started, then look at images of the lunch and see right there the transformation that has occurred.

OPPOSITE The bounty – purple waxy potatoes, some kipflers, radishes, dutch carrots and my warrigal greens pesto.

BELOW Cornflowers from the garden decorate the table.

Jon, our 'go to' man for advice, on his way to the spring lunch.

Starting Your Own Community Garden

There is a wealth of advice available online about community gardens and how to get started. Here are just a few of the sites you might want to check out:

- The Australian City Farms and Community Gardens Network, an informal organisation that helps connect and advise people interested in community gardens. See www.communitygarden.org.au for some helpful factsheets, as well as a host of other useful information and links
- City of Sydney Council, which has a great publication called *Getting Started in Community Gardening*, available at www.cityofsydney.nsw.gov.au/community/participation/community-gardens
- Cultivating Community, an organisation based in Melbourne, which is best-known for its work supporting community gardens in inner-city public housing estates – see www.cultivatingcommunity.org.au
- Community Centres SA, which has published a booklet on community gardens, entitled *Growing Community: Starting and Nurturing Community Gardens*, available at www.communitycentressa.asn.au/sector-development/community-gardens.

If you are thinking about starting your own community garden, here are a few tips.

CREATING YOUR OWN COMMUNITY

The most important thing is to get together a group of like-minded people with a shared vision for the community garden, and the determination to make it happen. Print off some flyers and do a small letterbox-drop in your neighbourhood, and place ads in the local newspaper, and on noticeboards in your local library or shopping centre.

TOP Brother Mick shovelling soil into the new beds.

BOTTOM Nick Collier helping with the initial installation.

We were very lucky with our committee – our founding members included a landscape architect, a horticulturist, a marketing guru, an urban designer, a project manager and an ex-accountant. But don't be put off if you don't have this skill set in your own community – the main thing to look for is people who are passionate about the project and prepared to work hard.

Once you have your group, organise a series of social days to get together and work out a management plan, setting out proposed funding, management, membership and insurance, as well as dealing with some of the nitty-gritty details, such as compost, waste disposal, rainwater tanks, storage, shelter and signage.

CHECK OUT OTHER COMMUNITY GARDENS

Do some practical research. Contact your local council or use the internet to locate community gardens near you, then go to see them, talk to the organisers and see how they do things, what worked and what didn't, and what obstacles they encountered along the way.

FIND A SITE

There are so many places which could be transformed into vibrant gardens – just open your eyes and look around. Look for vacant land, then find out who owns it and contact the owner about access. Use your imagination – how about your nature strip, or that sunny corner at the end of the street?

You could also approach your local council to see if it has any land you could use. Councils often have unkempt areas or dull, municipal plantings around the 'hood, and these days they are actively encouraging people to start community gardens. The City of Sydney Council has its own community garden policy (as do many other councils), and employs someone specifically to help co-ordinate community gardens.

If your local council doesn't have something like this in place, they should at least be able to point you in the right direction. Hassle them!

You might be able to set up a vegie garden on some unused land at a local school, or there may be an existing vegie patch you could become involved with. A few years ago I helped Darlinghurst Public School set up their vegie garden, and I loved gardening and interacting with the kids.

My experience with school gardens is that parents are often time-poor, and if you can lend a hand in any way you will be most welcome (you might have to sign a clearance for working with children before you begin.) Stephanie Alexander's Kitchen Garden Foundation (www.kitchengardenfoundation.org.au), a wonderful organisation set up to help teach kids how to grow and cook their own produce, has inspired many schools to set up kitchen gardens. Many are looking for volunteers, and if you are having trouble setting up your own community garden, this is one way to become involved.

SITE ASSESSMENT

Once you have found a place for your garden, you will need to do a thorough site assessment, looking at things like soil condition, water availability, weather conditions, which are the sunny spots and which are more shady, which parts exposed and which are more sheltered. You also need to consider existing plants and structures, like paths, fences, seating, and decide if you want to keep them.

DESIGNING THE GARDEN

You might need help from an expert to design a garden plan, working out what you will plant and where.

On page 154 you will see the garden plan that we had for our community garden. The layout you choose really depends on the space you have available. As I mentioned earlier, we used circular, raised garden beds to maximise space in our triangular-shaped area. Rectangular or square areas might work better for you.

Raised beds are preferable, as they allow everyone (young and old) easy access to the crops and also provide other benefits, such as improving drainage and soil quality. You can make beds quite easily and cheaply from old hardwood sleepers (don't use treated pine, as it's treated with chemicals and toxic for garden beds). Keep the design simple and ensure there is good access between the beds, wide enough for wheelchairs, prams, kids and dogs.

You will also need to think about how the garden is to be used. Will there be individual allotments for people and organisations, or will everyone share in the labour and the harvest? Or will it be a mixture of both? In our garden, different people are responsible for gardening and maintaining particular parts of the garden, but all members share equally in the bounty.

TOP Yours truly.

BOTTOM Kati lends a hand.

SPONSORSHIP AND SUPPORT

It's good for local businesses to be involved with community projects, so it is definitely worthwhile to make contact and invite their support. As well as seeking cash donations, be creative. Ask local gardening companies to lend a hand with horticultural knowledge if your group is lacking in this area. Ask your local landscape supply company if they can donate soil or other materials, or supply them at cost. You could also approach the larger companies who grow seeds or seedlings, to see if they are open to sponsoring your space.

You might also like to approach your local council for funding assistance – we were lucky enough to get a generous matching grant from the City of Sydney.

It's important to acknowledge any support you receive; advertise it on your noticeboard, in emails or flyers, and let your neighbours know what each organisation has done.

Sponsorship is paramount in any community garden, and we are very lucky to have an arrangement with natural cosmetics company, Burt's Bees, who the Council sent our way. They make a generous annual donation, and also help out at our working bees. In return, Burt's uses the garden for product launches, aligning them with a very worthwhile social project. It's a win-win – it's good for their corporate image, and we have the funds we need to maintain and develop the garden.

Tenacious Tamara, in charge of sponsorship, also obtained all of our original planter beds without charge, as well as procuring concrete pipes, worm farms, compost bins and many other essential things.

Sponsorship is vital for the ongoing financial health of our garden, allowing us to keep membership fees to just $20 a year, which covers everything, including seeds, fertilisers and plants. We are now looking at ways of making the garden financially self-supporting, by offering short courses in organic gardening for vegie gardens.

BORING RED TAPE!

Although it sounds a bit tedious, it's a good idea to have a members' agreement, dealing with issues like how decisions are made, membership, and who's responsible for what. Some of the websites I mention on page 164 have examples of agreements you can adapt.

In our case, the Council gave us use of the space for one year but after that we had to enter into a five-year licence agreement. To do that, we had to become incorporated, which meant we had to have a more formal agreement, called a constitution. It sounds exhausting just reading it. Basically, we needed to have a formal structure, hold regular committee meetings and an annual general meeting, and meet other requirements so we could obtain public liability insurance to protect us from possible litigation. Our constitution is a modified version of one available for incorporated associations on the website of New South Wales Fair Trading.

OPPOSITE The graffiti wall is constantly changing, giving the garden a sometimes macabre backdrop. Note the circular garden bed.

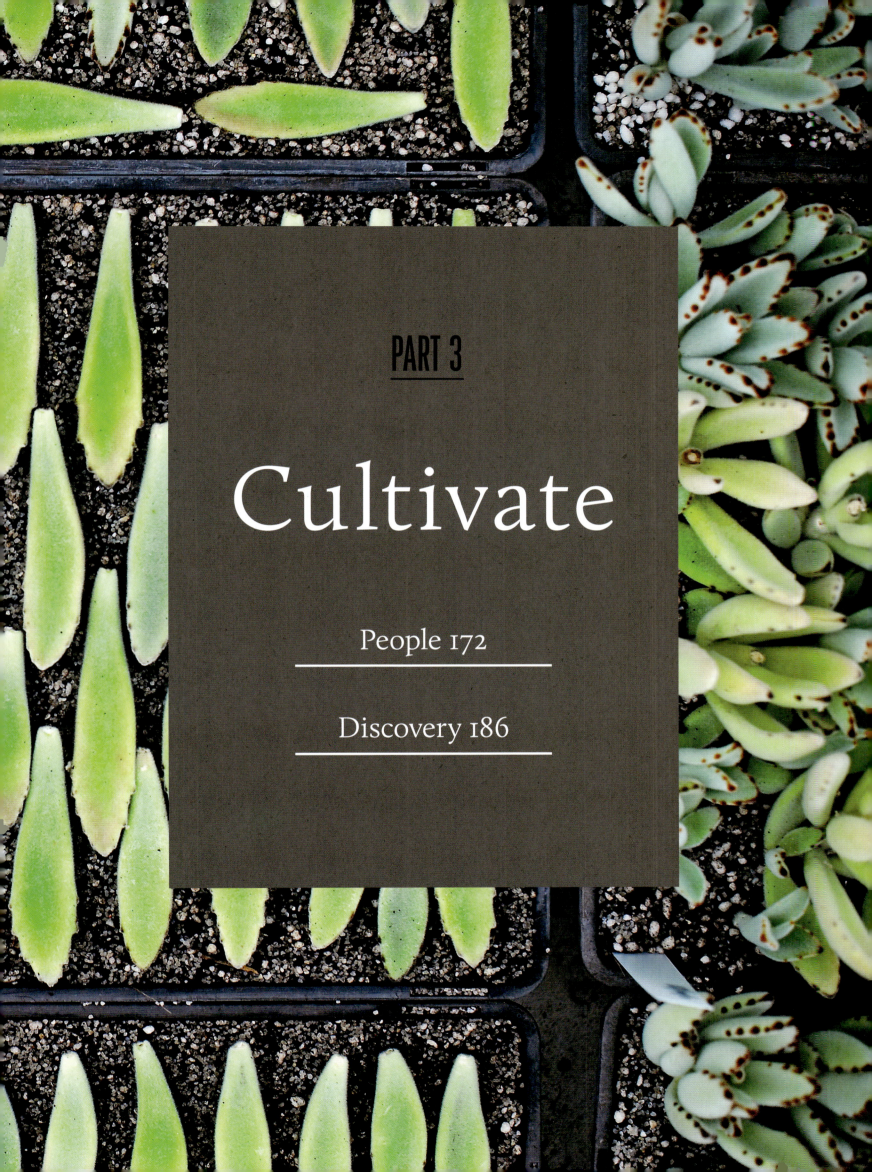

PART 3

Cultivate

People 172

Discovery 186

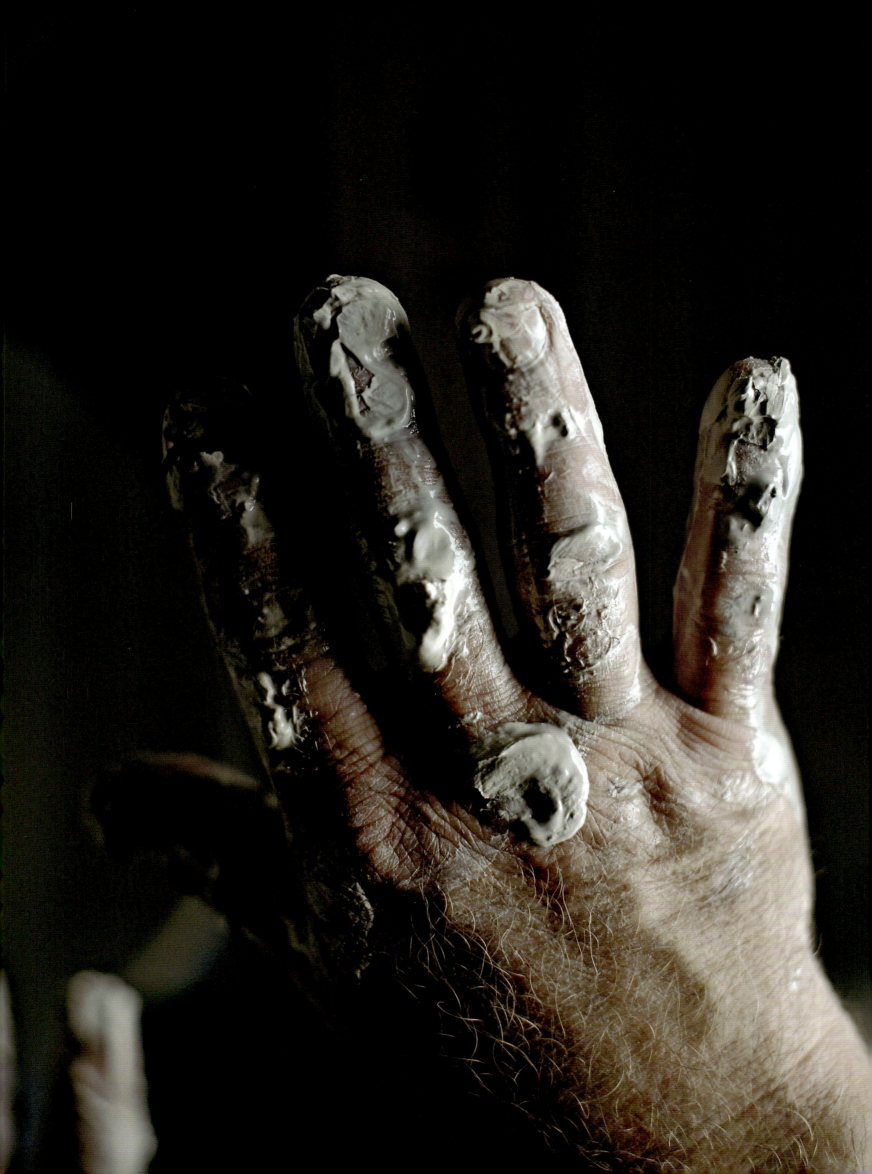

I want to introduce you to some of the people who help give our little business its personality. When I first started working for myself it was me, my van and a few tools. This was good for a short while, although I'm the sort of person who quickly gets bored with my own company; I thrive on working with and learning from others – it's essential for me. Today in my work life I find myself surrounded and supported by people whom I love working with.

I wouldn't have a business at all if it wasn't for these amazing people, some of whose stories I'd like to share with you. There is the Garden Life team itself, the backbone of the business, there are the growers and nurseries where we find our beautiful plants, and, finally, there are some outstanding local artisans whose work complements our own so well.

I cherish my relationships with these creative individuals who are masters of their craft, whether it's growing plants, creating organic sculpture or throwing pots. I like to think of Garden Life as a celebration of what can be achieved by working with others, whether it's colleagues, suppliers, clients, friends or even family!

Although it started out as purely a garden design buisness, Garden Life is now much more than that. I have always been interested in retail, so it was only a matter of time before I expanded from garden design into owning my own store, Garden Life, first in Darlinghurst and then in Redfern in inner-city Sydney. The larger premises have enabled us to stock a wider range of beautiful objects, and I have had a great time filling the store with treasures sourced from my overseas travels, as a result of relationships I have cultivated over the years.

My aim is for the store to be accessible and inspirational, and for it to give people ideas about how to create a space they love to be in.

CHAPTER 5

People

Working with others has been the key to having such an enjoyable and successful business. It is so rewarding and I know that I can run into trouble if I try to do everything myself. Garden Life wouldn't be what it is without the support of my brother, Mick, and our team of dedicated employees, and it is this collaboration that makes me want to get out of bed each morning. I also really value my relationship with the suppliers, growers and other skilled operators who help us do what we do, and I strongly believe that the business is successful because of this network of support.

The Garden Life Team

My brother Mick came out from the UK around the time that I was opening my first store in Darlinghurst, and I quickly roped him into helping with the business. At first he was just lending a hand, but his role soon turned into much more than that and after a few years, we became equal partners. Mick now has a massive role; I absolutely couldn't do it without him, and wouldn't want to do it with anyone else. It certainly has been a process of trusting and letting go for this self-declared control freak!

For the past few years I have also worked closely with my creative right-hand man, Nick Vale, who has injected a wonderful vibrancy and freshness into our work. Ebo manages the retail side of the business, and his energy and offbeat sense of humour are legendary – clients love him! We wouldn't have a business without our clients, and I feel blessed to work with some truly lovely people. Allowing someone into your personal space to design your garden involves a good degree of trust and patience, and many clients have turned into friends.

OPPOSITE The two Richards – me with one of the gardeners, Richard Seddon.

ABOVE LEFT I couldn't do what I do without my brother and business partner, Mick.

ABOVE RIGHT With Nick, creative right-hand man.

BELOW Ebo and friend. Ebo has been an invaluable part of the business for the past ten years.

Collaborators

One of the most enjoyable aspects of my job is heading out to see our growers, to source and select our plants. What makes it so special? I think it's the road trip, getting out of the office, onto the open road, being out of phone range and basically going shopping on a big scale! It seems to happen at a slower pace than the other aspects of the business, and sourcing beautiful plants, seeing what's around really keeps me stimulated. It's also a great opportunity to have a catch-up, a cup of tea and a good yarn.

Without fail, Mick and I visit a growers' market each month, where we connect with a wide range of growers who come from all over the country to sell their plants to Sydney landscapers, designers and retailers. It's an early start, up at 4.30 a.m., grabbing some early caffeine from Bar Coluzzi in Darlinghurst. The markets open at 6 a.m. and the early bird definitely catches the worm – anything unusual needs to be claimed fast!

I always have one list of plants we need for the shop and one for the gardens we are currently working on or are about to install. I find this plant selection a

creative process in itself – sometimes a plant will pop out at me that I hadn't previously considered, and I often make decisions depending on what's looking good on the day.

After visiting the markets, it's time to go and visit the guys who don't sell at the markets, the growers, who are gurus at growing particular plants. Nurserymen and women are salt-of-the-earth, straightforward characters - I'm not sure what it is, perhaps their connection to the land and their plants. There is something deeply satisfying about visiting them. They are always a mine of information, with great knowledge about the plants they grow, and they are the first people I will ask for advice about different species and their suitability for what I have in mind.

Finally, I am lucky to have worked with some amazing artisans whose work enhances my own.

Here is a snapshot of a few of my favourite suppliers.

OPPOSITE Plant labels ready to accompany the plants when they go to market.

BELOW, CLOCKWISE FROM LEFT Slightly chaotic greenhouse; patterns are everywhere; huge variegated Mauritius hemp.

Paul and Gigi Modde

Paul and Gigi first arrived in Australia in 1965 by plane from Belgium, and spent their first ten months in Australia in a detention centre with other English immigrants. Once they were released, Paul started his own landscaping business, growing plants on the side. Conifer gardens were becoming popular at the time, and he started his nursery with over eighty different varieties. When conifer sales dropped, Paul and Gigi started growing AZALEAS, JAPANESE and ENGLISH BOX and other more general lines. Gigi also discovered a passion for growing bonsai.

One of their specialities is the very unusual hanging succulent RHIPSALIS. These are bizarre-looking plants, actually EPIPHYTIC CACTUS, with long, green cascading spaghetti-like stems. Perfect for spilling over walls and out of hanging planters, their drought-hardiness makes them a very versatile plant, which I like to use to soften harsh walls.

Graeme and Wendy Twaddell

Graeme and Wendy ran a landscaping business and retail nursery in Beecroft for about twenty years, before closing it down to focus on growing succulents. Today they have a vast array of succulents, **CLIVIAS** and a few orchids on their Dural property.

Graeme's old A-frame timber glasshouses are home to the most wildly exotic succulents I have ever seen. One of Graeme's clients is so obsessed that he flies over from Korea to handpick some **ECHEVERIAS** before flying back and waiting for his booty to arrive by air. Of all the nurseries I visit, Graeme's is one of my favourites, and each time I visit I'm reminded of my parents' old timber greenhouse back in Yorkshire; it's just like putting on a favourite old jumper with patched elbows.

There is a real character called Troy who works at the nursery. Troy is a master at succulent propagation, and each time I visit he will be sitting in the same plastic chair in the full sun, scissors in one hand, gently snipping the plants with utmost patience and diligence. The trays of newly propagated plant material will be laid out in a wonderfully regimented manner and the leaves and stems will be massed in their trays creating amazing patterns and contrasting blocks of shapes and colours – a bit like some layered artwork by Rosalie Gascoigne.

One of Graeme and Wendy's beautiful old greenhouses.

Philip Pratt

Philip runs a nursery from his farm between Peats Ridge and Wollombi. He is the 'Edward Scissorhands' of topiary growers, and his property is a sight to behold. There is a strong sense of prevailing order, with his perfectly manicured specimens beautifully laid out and surrounded by neatly trimmed grass. There is something very meditative about walking around the parallel rows of clipped topiary.

Philip must be a patient man, as some of his specimens are over fourteen years old. He ranks the Japanese as the best gardeners in the world and their influence on him is clear, especially in the topiary CLOUD TREES he creates from CHINESE JUNIPER (*Juniperus chinensis* 'Kaizuka' also called 'Keteleeri') that he clips so masterfully. Phil also grows majestic, bushy magnolias, big thick balls, cones and spirals of JAPANESE BOX (*Buxus microphylla*) and various species of podocarpus, including the NATIVE PLUM PINE (*Podocarpus elatus*), which is a great conifer for a shady spot. In contrast to the topiary, he also produces a host of architectural specimen plants such as GYMEA LILY (*Doryanthes excelsia*) and the RUSH-LEAF BIRD OF PARADISE (*Strelitzia juncea*).

Phil loves his plants, but his real passion is for the 1971 Ford Fairmont XY that sits in his garage. He is a founding member of the Mangrove Mountain Muscle Car Club – during the week, he is a peaceful, quietly spoken nurseryman, but on the weekend he turns into a fully-fledged petrol-head!

Tracey Deep

Tracey has a natural talent for working with flowers and natural materials, and I'm a huge fan of her bold work. She creates the most beautiful sculptures from all manner of objects – everything from bra underwires, old horse bridle leather, tarred ropes or an unusual collection of organic stems, and her truly unique pieces look great on any wall.

Over the past few years we have worked together on several projects – Tracey's sculptures complement our gardens beautifully. Because art is so personal, I usually just put our client and Tracey in touch with each other and let them work out the solution together.

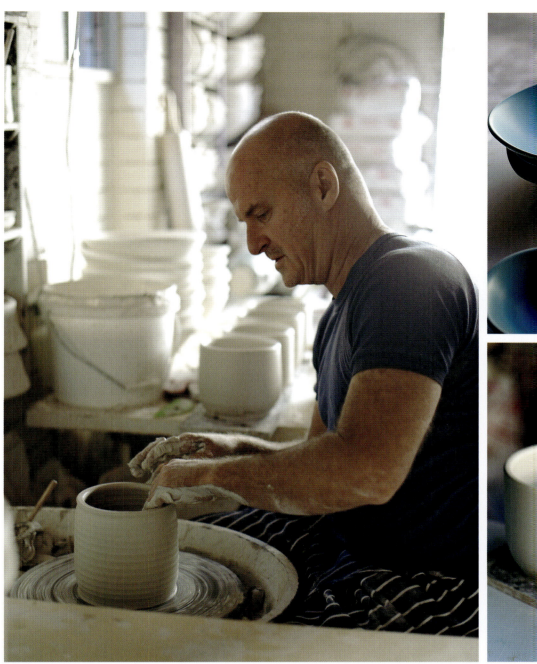

Dave Edmonds

I approached Dave, a local ceramicist, about producing a range of small pots and planters for us after seeing his range of dinnerware. The unique satin-matte finish of his beautifully crafted bowls and plates just makes you want to touch them all the time. I wanted pots that could be used inside as well as outside, and Dave adapted his dinnerware surface, and has now been supplying us with fantastic hand-thrown pots for some time.

I love the simplicity of Dave's work; his earthenware pots are so warm and tactile, with a beautiful, soft glow. The simple shapes let the plants do the talking, framing them like works of art. I especially love seeing his hanging planters planted with the **RHIPSALIS CACTUS** that Paul and Gigi grow for us – it's a perfect marriage. His planters also contrast well with the simple flower pots I bring in from Turkey – I like mixing up his slick, smooth shapes with the rough terracotta.

CHAPTER 6

Discovery

As the garden design business continued to grow, I started to think about combining my love of horticulture and design with my love of retail and Garden Life, the store, was born. In my quest to fill it with beautiful pots and other objects, I soon started to source merchandise as I travelled, so I could offer my clients unique, hand-selected pieces.

My Travels

We all love to travel – there is the constant stimulation, as you find beauty in both the simple and the extravagant, and you watch things grow and take shape, maturing and changing, as life unfolds. I started travelling to source goods for the store about five years ago, and I now do four or five trips a year.

The last few years have taken me to France, Turkey, India, Sri Lanka, China and, more recently, Vietnam. Unsurprisingly, hey, you know what? I love everything about it – the adventure, the change of routine, and, most of all, the people I meet. I find random meetings and exchanges of energy are as enjoyable as finding some beautiful new piece or stumbling across a real gem of a supplier. It is in these simple interactions with locals that I feel connected and energised, especially if I'm travelling alone.

It sounds clichéd, but as I travel, I try to keep my eyes open to every possibility. As part of my personal, spiritual beliefs, I feel that there is some kind of divine inspiration and energy out there that I can tap into. The things I'm meant to find seem to have a way of presenting themselves. As I expand my travel horizons, I am slowly filling the store with unique objects with different textures, shapes and stories. These gorgeous old pieces from around the world add another layer to our more contemporary pieces, and it is this blending of the contemporary and the traditional which seems to work so well.

My travels influence my design work as well. Over the years I have visited many gardens, from Manhattan and the UK to Rajasthan, and they all influence and inspire my work – whether it is materials used in a floor at the Topkapi Palace in Istanbul, or a wall built by the brilliant Andy Goldsworthy in the Yorkshire Sculpture Park. I might check out the meadow plantings at the High Line in New York, or study how the herbaceous borders are composed in the gardens of Sissinghurst Castle. I think everything I see goes somewhere upstairs into my creative head and comes out here and there when required!

OPPOSITE A typical street scene in Galle, Sri Lanka.

ABOVE LEFT I love train travel in India, especially overnight.

ABOVE RIGHT A colourful character at the Delhi flower markets.

BELOW Hunting for antique doors.

INDIA

India is a massively rich source of all manner of goods and chattels and I love travelling there. Ancient crafts such as blacksmithing, marble- and stone-carving (which have died out in Western countries) are handed down from father to son, and are still thriving. You never know how you might come across useful information, either. Once I was in a clothes shop in Delhi, and the designer and I got talking about our respective businesses, and he told me of a place that specialised in antique brass. This priceless information that came from a chance meeting is precisely how it can happen when you are travelling and interacting with local people. One connection in a store leads to a new friendship and the possibility of sourcing some gorgeous new pieces (or rather old pieces) for my store.

There are all kinds of ways to hunt for wares in India. There are some large, well-organised export places, but I much prefer to hunt around for smaller traders. This might take me to the dusty old basement of somebody's house, to see the collection of brass planters they have been collecting for the past twenty years. The selection process takes some time, and it is important for me to be relaxed, thorough and unhurried, as there is usually a lot to look through before I come across exactly what I'm looking for. I have had my share of wild goose chases, involving long trips in weird forms of transport to places I would rather not be. But every lead, story and bit of information needs to be considered because it might just be as good as it sounds.

SRI LANKA

Vanessa, a friend of mine, is Sri Lankan, and it was her stories of the amazing food and friendly people that planted the seed of my interest in this small island to the south of India. A chap called Geoffrey Bawa is the other reason Sri Lanka was on my mind – he was Sri Lanka's best-known, most prolific architect. Trained in London, he paid as much attention to exteriors and landscape design as he did to interiors, and he connected the two seamlessly.

Bawa's work still resonates deeply, and when I booked to stay in his former residence in Colombo I was really excited at the prospect of immersing myself in his world. The humble townhouse towards the end of a narrow suburban cul-de-sac straddles interior and exterior space, and his trademark connection with the outdoors flows through the house. Light wells are planted with lush tropical foliage open to the elements. In one of them a large, swollen tree trunk just rises out of the floor, and in another a mass of **RHAPIS PALMS** adds greenery to the crisp interior.

Hungry for more inspiration from Bawa, I headed to his country residence, Lunaganga, a sprawling estate sitting above a large lake just inland from Bentota, on the south-west coast. The magnificent garden there evolved over forty years. There is a funky contemporary outdoor living room with Bawa's trademark modernist built-in sofas. The garden next to this room is dominated by an expansive frangipani tree, planted for impact at the corner of the terrace. Selected branches of its twisted, tortured limbs must have had weights attached when the tree was young, to make them low-growing and horizontal, and over the years it has been perfectly crafted to fit the space. It truly is a bonsai of Bawa proportions.

Beyond this tree, the lawn falls gently away to low, colonnaded retaining walls, on top of which stand traditional Italianate figures. The gardens drop down to the edges of the lake and there are a series of rice paddies and old fruit orchards on its banks. Low, moss-covered stone walls and wide steps leading down to the water, combined with the formal layout of the adjacent rice fields, give the space a bizarre feeling of Lake Como meets Ubud.

OPPOSITE The sublime entry hall to Geoffrey Bawa's home where we stayed in Colombo. I love the way the swollen tree trunk rises out of the floor.

BELOW Crisp white contrasts with sculpture, antiques and earthy elements.

BOTTOM Ornate door to Geoffrey Bawa's bedroom, thought to be by Australian artist Donald Friend, a regular visitor to Lunaganga.

TOP The immense frangipani at Geoffrey Bawa's country retreat Lunuganga. The branches must have had weights attached when they were younger, to keep them low. It is like a giant bonsai.

BOTTOM Humble prayer.

TOP Water lotus in a pond at Geoffrey Bawa's old offices, now a café and retail space in Colombo.

BOTTOM The magnificent garden at Lunaganga has evolved over forty years.

Through a local contact I met a collector named Charith, and we drove to look at his stock of beautiful old Lankan furniture and other collectables in various warehouses around Colombo. The pieces had a distinct colonial influence, with simple, classic lines, and good scale and proportion and I bought some lovely old brass pieces, including some polished brass bowls. Somewhere else I came across a collection of unusual, decorative brass pieces that caught my eye. They were exactly the sort of thing I was hoping to find, unique pieces with character, depth, and significance.

On this trip I also found some beautiful, intricately cut brass oil burners, used in the home to worship Lakshmi, the Hindu goddess of wealth and prosperity. Another striking ornamental item, a large brass sculpture from Jaffna, was used to surround and protect my favourite Hindu god, Ganesh (the remover of obstacles). I also found lots of old ceramic jars, once filled with acid and used as early batteries, which work beautifully as simple vases. Large, old copper cooking pots with strong, simple lines are perfect for planting and I can use them in compositions with more contemporary planters. Each and every one of these hand-picked pieces will add unique quality, depth and energy to someone's house back in Australia.

Finding pieces for the store was really a bonus, because I had such a great time just exploring, tasting and being inspired by how people like Geoffrey Bawa have lived. I so enjoy hunting around in these far-flung places for items I truly hope people will love as much as I do. The pieces I selected in India and Sri Lanka have added a certain richness to the shop; there is such history and depth in the brass, copper and marble objects, many made by hand, using traditional methods that have been used for centuries.

It is great when the items I have lovingly hand-selected overseas arrive at the shop. As soon as I received the pieces from Sri Lanka, I started unpacking the crates with crowbars and diving into the wooden boxes filled with masses of shredded paper. It was just like Christmas – on steroids!

TOP Creeping fig on a statue.

ABOVE Heavenly Buddha.

RIGHT Beautifuly laid-out offerings to Buddha at a roadside shrine.

OPPOSITE Selecting from Charith's amazing collection of furniture and other objects.

TURKEY

I first came across Marea in about 1998 when she pulled up outside Parterre, the store I was managing at the time. She lifted the back door of her old van and it was stuffed full of amazing pots, urns and various objects she had bought from a family of four brothers on a recent trip to Turkey. Like a travelling merchant of yesteryear, she was driving round to various businesses offering her wares; how very old-school! Although I didn't know it at the time, we would later become firm business friends, and she was to play a key part in my business.

When I opened my own store, I started buying pieces from Marea myself. Her warehouse in the inner-west was a sight to behold. She had a good eye, and she selected well. With each shipment there were always stories about the goods she found on her travels, all made from natural, earthy materials. There were pieces in every shape and size, made from terracotta, ceramics, stone and timber, and almost all of them had once had a practical use, whether as a butter churn, flour drum or even a plough.

I greatly admired gentle Marea, and grew very fond of her – her travels sounded so exotic. She was wiry and lean, and handled huge pieces with ease, rolling up her sleeves and getting stuck in. She was truly a one-woman business, who created a loyal following over the years. We did business together for at least a decade, until Marea had to shut down her wholesale business due to ill health. Sadly, she passed away not long after that.

After a time, I began to think more about Turkey, and Marea's stories about the family she had grown so fond of there, and on one of my visits to the UK to see my family, I decided to make a side-trip to Turkey to see what I could find. I didn't really know where to start; the only information I had about the business Marea dealt with was an old piece of paper with a phone number scrawled on it.

I contacted an old friend, Chris Hall, who was living in Turkey and set off there for a short trip. Istanbul is only four hours from Yorkshire by air, but when I arrived it felt more like four million miles – what a marvellous culture shock! The ancient city hummed with an energy all of its own. It is truly a melting pot of the East and West.

One of my first stops was the bustling Grand Bazaar, or Kapali Carsi, in the heart of the old city. The fifteenth-century market, with its sixty-one covered streets, is one of the largest enclosed markets in the world, and it was hard not to get lost in the maze of small lanes and alleyways. I loved the crumbling plaster and patterned, brick-vaulted ceilings; the whole place had a mad, vibrant energy all its own. I stumbled upon a stack of vibrant, orange Ikat bowls from Kazakhstan. The colour caught my eye in the dusty window, and I spent an hour or so rummaging through, selecting my favourites from the Afghani trader. I also found some heavily decorated porcelain plates celebrating the Kazakhstani participation in the Olympic Games (year unknown). I love a mad, unexpected find like that, of something totally left of centre, which I can bring back to the store for show and tell (and sale).

Stuffing my backpack full, I continued my search, discovering a tiny textile shop selling intricate, handwoven silk and velvet cushions from Uzbekistan. (I'm becoming a big fan of the 'Stans!). Generally, I'm not big on highly decorative, heavily patterned fabrics, but I loved how the fabric caught the light and how luxurious it looked. I went inside, and ended up sitting down on the floor and talking textiles for a couple of hours over some wicked Turkish coffee with the two brothers who ran the shop. I love learning not just about what people are selling, but their own personal stories, how they came to be doing what they do. Turkey is still a land of the family business, of being born into a particular trade, learning the ropes from the

OPPOSITE TOP Workers lift my hand-selected flower pots onto a trolley, ready to be packed.

OPPOSITE CENTRE Antique marble mortars.

OPPOSITE BOTTOM LEFT Yusuf, with his kind eyes.

OPPOSITE BOTTOM RIGHT A stack of old water jars.

ABOVE Antique urns in the store.

father and continuing the tradition. I selected about twenty cushions for the shop.

Realising I had a fluent Turkish interpreter at my disposal, I asked Chris to call the phone number of Marea's contact for me. It turns out I had the right number and the right people. They were located right in the middle of Turkey, a short flight away, and they said they would be very pleased to see me. The next day I flew into a small regional airport, where I was met by Husseyin, a marvellously moustachioed member of the family. We drove for about an hour through the arid countryside, as I became increasingly excited about what I might see.

We stopped at an office in the village where I met Yusuf, the oldest of the four brothers, who had taken over the business after their father died. Yusuf's smiling welcome was so warm; his wise old face lighting up when he spoke. The humble space was crammed full of a mad collection of small curios: dusty oil lamps, worn wooden ladles and spoons, rusty, hand-forged chains and hooks, old brass bells, ceramic olive oil jugs, an assortment of cooking pots and bundles of huge prayer beads.

We headed to their warehouse at the edge of town, pulling up at the rusted gates of a yard containing a collection of ramshackle old buildings. As we started to walk around, doors were opened, lights were turned on, and it quickly became apparent that I was in the middle of a truly amazing collection. There were rows and rows of antique planters, terracotta urns, weird and wonderful agricultural vessels, stone mortars, old machinery, delicate hand-painted ceramic vases and Ottoman-empire brass candlesticks. It was honestly like arriving at Ali Baba's cave! What I really loved was hearing the stories behind the pieces, each of which once had a practical use – whether it was a wheat thrasher pulled behind a horse, or a tree trunk hollowed out by hand and used as a butter churn. I loved imagining where each piece might have been, and who it might have belonged to.

I chose some amazing old dough bowls and boards, as well as some massive old tree trunks once used for storing wheat. I also bought some weathered wheat threshers and some Greek jars which would have been two to three hundred years old. I quietly said a heartfelt 'thank you' to Marea – I'm so grateful to her for bringing these remarkable people into my life, and I think she would be happy to know that I am carrying on her tradition of bringing their wonderful objects back to Australia.

ABOVE A stack of olive baskets.

RIGHT White and blue limewashed pots.

OPPOSITE TOP Treasure!

OPPOSITE BOTTOM The wonderful family I met through Marea – Yusuf and his brothers Mustafa and Mehmet.

A FEW OF MY FAVOURITE THINGS

Space doesn't allow me to mention all of the wonderful pieces I have brought back from my travels, and where they have found homes in Australia, but here are some favourites.

URNS FROM TURKEY

I found a particularly beautiful old urn in Turkey a couple of years ago. The family I buy from kept it for me, as I had asked them to look out for any stand-out larger pieces. It is about 300 years old, and was used for storing olive oil. From an aesthetic point of view, there is something just so beautiful and simple in its shape, and then what about the history? Where has it been? How many people have owned it or come across it in the past?

I had been on the lookout for a few large urns to use as statement pieces around the outside of the home of clients in Point Piper, and bought this specifically for them (see pages 12–27 for more on their garden). These large, original pieces add instant weight, texture and scale wherever they are placed, and this one sits perfectly at the corner of the lower terrace.

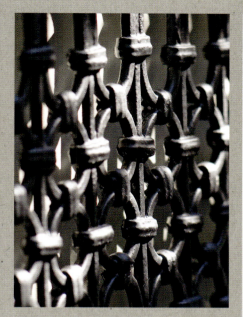

IRON JALI SCREENS FROM INDIA

Iron jali window screens have been around in India for hundreds of years. They are beautiful pieces, made from wrought iron, surrounded by heavy, wooden frames in intricate patterns. As well as looking good, they provide privacy and security, letting in the sunlight yet deterring intruders. You see a lot of them in India on the older, more traditional buildings.

I asked someone in India to make me a series of new ones in a simple pattern for the store. I could see that they would make their presence felt by adding interest to bland walls. You don't often see this sort of intricate detail, and the repetition of the panels creates a strong look. These days we see more and more vertical walls in our urban environment, and these pieces add character, charm and personality.

When some clients asked for help with the atrium of their townhouse in Walsh Bay, I wanted to use the new jalis, as I knew she would love their delicate, handmade aesthetic. I just had to convince him that we could rustproof them so they would not stain his wall – and we did. Read more about their place on pages 108–111.

RECYCLED RUBBER POTS FROM VIETNAM

The Vietnamese are skilled craftspeople when it comes to making baskets (and many other things), and very resourceful in the way they reuse materials. When I was in Ho Chi Minh City, I saw people making baskets out of old car and scooter tyres (if you have ever been there, you'll understand there are quite a few of those flying around everywhere!). They are tough, light and look cool, with a very earthy feel. I arranged for some to be made for us, to use as planters. The stitched seams give them a handcrafted edge, and their clean lines make them perfect for contemporary spaces.

When I was reworking parts of a garden in Paddington, and looking for some edgy planters with a handmade element, these pots fitted the bill perfectly.

YOGHURT POTS FROM TURKEY

On a visit to Turkey a few years ago I found a selection of large pots which instantly caught my eye. They were made from a soft volcanic stone, similar to pumice, and were used to make yoghurt. As with most of the old pieces that I bring in, it was the texture and shape I loved the most. A simple shape like this can fit into contemporary settings with ease – it is the imperfect, weathered look that makes them fit in so well, adding instant character. I used one of these pots at a client's place in Newtown (see pages 104–107). It's hard to say how old it was, but my guess is anywhere between 100 to 200 years old.

TULIP URNS FROM INDIA

I loved these urns as soon as I saw them at a marble-carver's in northern India. Each has been hand-carved from one piece of marble, and, though they weigh about 200 kilograms each, their lines are soft and graceful.

They are real 'hero' pieces, which make a bold statement. I installed some at a client's place in Rushcutters Bay. It is a rich, textured, formal courtyard with many layers, and the urns are perfectly at home here in their luxe surroundings. They suit soft, flowing plantings best, so we massed them with BRAZILIAN WALKING IRIS (*Neomarcia gracilis*), which arch over, reflecting the style of the urn.

The Store

My retail store acts as the beating heart of the business, where it all comes together. Everything in the store comes from the relationships I've cultivated with growers, suppliers and artisans from all over the world. I like to think of it as a space everyone can enjoy – our staff, our customers and our community. My aim is for people to walk into the store, soak up its good energy, and enjoy the various plants and pieces we have collected from around the world.

First we have our plants, each of which is hand-picked from the growers I talk about in chapter 5. I try to carry a few great plants for both indoors and outside, and I'm always on the lookout for something unusual. I like to have a few larger house plants in stock as hero plants to make an instant statement, as well as smaller, potted specimens which make good gifts or can be used around the home. Having plants in the store creates good energy, and allows us to create simple compositions demonstrating how plants can be used in and around the garden and home.

About half of our business is selling pots and planters, and they come in all shapes, sizes, colours and textures. I try to offer a range of pots that work with every style of home, whether it's an uber-chic inner-city pad, an earthy country farmhouse, or a large commercial rooftop.

We design a lot of our pots and planters ourselves. As I mentioned, we have designed a range of smaller planters with Dave Edmonds, a local ceramicist renowned for his smooth satin glaze and soft organic forms (see page 185). On a larger scale, we have worked with a company in northern New South Wales to develop a range of large, lightweight concrete planters called bullet pots (these are the large white pots we used on the rooftop of the Australian Film Television and Radio School – see pages 76–83).

I am always on the lookout for interesting pieces with a connection to nature, which stand alone as beautiful objects. So, in the store you might see anything from a stack of orange porcelain bowls from Kazakhstan to a beautiful piece of Australian timber from a supplier in the Riverina, who delivers weather-beaten pieces of eucalypt to us tied to the back of his old car (quite a sight!).

Some of the lovely old pieces from India, Sri Lanka and Turkey, with their rich histories, contrast beautifully with our slicker, more contemporary pieces. I try to combine the rough with the smooth, the yin with the yang, the perfect with the imperfect – a bit like what I do with my garden design.

As I style the store, I like to play around with all the bits and pieces and just see what works and what doesn't as I try to get it 'just right' (until the next time). I want people to come into the store, feel welcome and just have a great experience, whether they buy something or not. One of my favourite local characters is Janet (the elder) (read more of her story on page 159). One day she took me aside and said, 'I feel very proud of this place. I feel like I belong here.' That is just how I want my customers to feel. Hopefully, they will also be inspired about how to best utilise their indoor or outdoor space and make it their own.

Final Thoughts

My aim with this book is to inspire people to look at their outdoor space with fresh eyes. I hope I have demonstrated that there are no set rules for creating the outdoor space around you, that it's more about making it yours, putting your stamp and personality on it.

Feel confident to explore all options and make decisions, even if sometimes you make mistakes. Start small, one step at a time, and have a go yourself – and if this all feels too hard, come and find us and we can help you!

As much as I wanted to write about the gardens we create, I also wanted to encourage people to think about how they live, how they want to live and how they relate to their community. My experience with growing food has brought me joy and connection with so many people – and as I write this, I realise that there's still so much I have to learn, that I really only know a little. It's my belief that growing our own food is healing on so many levels, and I hope this will become much more the norm in the near future.

I'm looking forward to more travels and adventure, to exploring more ground, to meeting new people in faraway places, as well as round the corner. For I feel that it's within our 'garden life' that we can find out a little about ourselves, and possibly a little more about each other.

Acknowledgements

This book is the sum of so many efforts by so many different people in my life.

I want to thank sincerely the Garden Life team past and present, without whom none of this would be possible. In particular, thank you to the current diehards Nick, Ebo, Josh, Carole, Karen, Lewis, Ana, Lauria, Mark, Kiwi Rich and Elicia.

To Twig Café for providing our clients with beautiful food and great coffee.

My wonderfully capable and patient GL partner in crime, Mick. I feel very lucky that we can work together as well as being brothers. I couldn't have done this without you, and I'm so thankful you are part of it.

I am very grateful to the loyal, dedicated shop customers who continually support our business, as well as clients past and present who trust us to help them with their gardens – big and small. I'd like to acknowledge in particular the following, who have made their gardens available to us for this project:

Linda and David Penn, Rob Schwamberg and Andrea Duff, Clive Magowan, Robert and Annabelle Hansen, Ruth Stockman, Mark Wood and Richard Baker, Sandra Levy, Del Kathryn Barton and Chris Plater, Clark Butler and Louise Herron, Helen Hendry, Paul Sinclair and Ben David.

To Jon and the many dedicated members of the James Street Reserve Community Garden, who have transformed that little corner into a thriving, energetic microcosm of goodness.

The team at Penguin Lantern. Julie Gibbs, I have so much gratitude to you for taking me on, believing in the story and being so patient. You pour the best tea. You also work with the best people. Katrina O'Brien for your lovely energy and direction, wonderful editor Nicole Abadee for your persistence, wise guidance and deft skill in making sense of my words. Mere thanks are not enough to the gifted Daniel New for creating such a truly beautiful book and fitting the jigsaw together – you are a craftsman!

Nick Watt, where do I start ?? Thank you for masterfully capturing our work and moments in your beautiful photography, for putting so much of yourself into this and for being a passionate believer right from the get-go. Thanks also for the best pho, honey, sandalwood soap and for being such a great travel buddy.

Neale Whitaker at *Belle* for initial introductions. Thank you to Cheryl Akle and Georgina Reid for their skill and advice right at the start, and to Jennifer Stackhouse for horticultural wisdom and verification at the end.

Dad, thanks for sowing radishes with me – I wish we had had the time to do more of it. Mum, for constantly creating in the garden and in the kitchen, for being of endless service to us kids and showing me how to be as well. I also want to mention my beautiful sisters, Kathy and Sally, and non-bio sisters Juzza and Babs – you all brighten up my life.

Greg, thanks for being there with me. I couldn't do this without you and your presence makes my life all the richer. Bill W for helping to make all things possible.

Index

Page references in italics are to photographs.

A
Acer japonicum 'Vitifolium' 61
Acer palmatum 22, 60
    'Bloodgood' 61
    'Sango-kaku' ('Senkaki') 61
Aeonium spp. *105, 107*
agapanthus (*Agapanthus praecox*) 66, 71, 122
agave 23, *41*, 42, 58, 60, 61, *64–5*, 86
    A. americana 'Mediopicta Alba' 37, *38–9*, 86
    A. attenuata 50, 60, 61, 86
    A. ocahui 45, *45*, 61, 86
    A. parryi 61
    A. victoriae-reginae 61
aloe 42, 84
    A. barberae 44, 84
    A. x *spinosissima* 110, *111*
Amy (author's niece) *136*
Arabian lilac (*Vitex trifolia* 'Purpurea') 55
architectural plants 43, 61, 73
'Aristocrat' ornamental pears 43
artichokes *132, 135*
atrium garden *108*
Australian City Farms and Community Gardens Network 164
Australian Film, Radio and Television School rooftop garden *45*, 76–83
Australian native violet (*Viola hederacea*) 116
azaleas 178

B
bamboo *38–9, 54, 89*, 100, *101, 156*
Bangalow palm (*Archontophoenix cunninghamiana*) 50, *59*, 116
banksias (*Banksia* spp.)
    B. integrifolia 73, 110
    B. robur 73
    B. serrata 73
basil *137*
Bawa, Geoffrey 191
Bawa garden in Sri Lanka *113, 190,* 191
beans 139
bearded iris (*Iris germanica*) 18, *25*, 42, 43
beetroot 139
begonias *58*, 61
Bellevue Hill formal garden 28–41, *113*
bird of paradise (*Strelitzia reginae*) *64–5*, 86 *see also* giant bird of paradise; rush-leaf bird of paradise
bird's nest fern (*Asplenium australasicum*) 50, 100
black bamboo (*Bambusa lako*) *103*, 110
black tupelo (*Nyssa sylvatica*) 32, *33*
Bland, Lesley and Quentin *144, 145,* 146
blue chalksticks (*Senecio serpens*) 73
blue jade (*Crassula* 'Blue Bird') 73
Boetz, Martin *148*, 149
borage *132*
Boston ivy (*Parthenocissus tricuspidata*) 37, *41, 78, 79*, 102
    'Lowii' 43, 60
box *see* English box; Japanese box
brassicas 145
Brazilian walking iris (*Neomarcia gracilis*) 86, *86*, 100, 116, 122, 201
broad beans 139
broccoli 139
broccolini 139
bromeliads *16, 36,* 42, *89, 123*
    Alcantarea imperialis 'Rubra' (Empress of Brazil) 32, *36, 41,* 42, 43, 100
    Billbergia 'Hallelujah' 37, 122
bronze-foliaged bromeliads (*Billbergia* 'Halleluja') 122
Buddha statue *194*
Burt's Bees 167
butterfly ginger (*Hedychium coronarium*) 116
Byron View Farm 46–59

C
Canary Island date palm (*Phoenix canariensis*) *113*
cane begonia (*Begonia coccinea*) 100, *101*
cardamom (*Alpinia nutans*) 100, 122
cardboard palm (*Zamia furfuracea*) 42, 43, 76, *83,* 87, *87*, 122
carrots 139–40, *160*
cast-iron plant (*Aspidistra elatior*) 18, 22, *23*, 42, 110
Casuarina glauca 'Cousin-It' 73
cavolo nero 141
celeriac *153*
celery 140
century plant (*Agave attenuata*) 50, 60, 61, 86
chillies 140
Chinese juniper (*Juniperus chinensis*) 'Kaizuka' ('Keteleeri') 32, 37, *41*, 43, 87, 96, 182

'Spartan' *16, 40*
Chinese tallow tree (*Sapium sebiferum*) 60
chives *154*
City of Sydney Council 153–4, 164–5
climbing plants 102
clippable plants 43, 61, 73
clivia (*Clivia miniata*) 179
coastal banksia (*Banksia integrifolia*) 110
coastal gardens 62–73
coastal hibiscus (*Hibiscus tiliaceus*) 73
coastal rosemary (*Westringia fruticosa*) 55, *59*, 61, *71*, 73
common jade (*Crassula ovata*) 22, 32, *33, 40*, 42, 43, *45*, 73, 84, 86, *92*, 96, *107*, 120, *122*
    'Gollum' (coral form) *89, 92,* 96, *97*
Community Centres SA 164
community gardens, starting your own 164–7
composition, creating 23, *24*, 88–9
composting 134
convolvulus 26
    C. sabatius 'Two Moons' *17,* 18, 43, 122
Cooks Co-op 149
coral form of common jade (*Crassula ovata* 'Gollum') *89, 92,* 96, *97*
coral plant *see* firecracker plant
Cos lettuce *132,* 132, 141
Cotyledon spp. 22, *82,* 96, *97*
    C. orbiculata 'Macrantha' 43
crazy paving *51,* 55, 60, 66, 72
creeping fig (*Ficus pumila*) 18, *19*, 43, 102
crepe myrtle (*Lagerstroemia indica* and *L. fauriei*) 50, 61
cucumbers 140
cycads (*Cycas revoluta*) 32, *33*, 43, 87, *113*

D
Darling Point townhouse garden *113,* 120–3
Dasylirion wheeleri ('sotol') *92*
Deep, Tracey 184
Dichondra spp.
    D. argentea 'Silver Falls' *45,* 87, *87,* 120, 122
    D. repens see kidney-weed
Dietes grandiflora see wild iris
donkey tail (*Sedum morganianum*) 18, *19*, 42
Doryanthes excelsa see Gymea lily
dragon tree (*Dracaena draco*) 71, 73, *89, 107*
dry stone walling *48–9, 54,* 55, 60, 72

dwarf Japanese pittosporum
(*Pittosporum tobira*)
'Miss Muffet' 43, 55, *58*, 60, 61, 73, 84, 96
'Wheelers Dwarf' 77

E

Ebo (manager) 175, *175*
echeveria (*Echeveria* spp.) 22, 60, 61, *70*, *82*, 179
Edible Garden Design 143
Edmonds, Dave *104*, 106, *119*, 185, *185*, 205
elephant bush (*Portulacaria afra*) 43
elephant ears (*Alocasia macrorrhizos*) 16, *16*, 116, 122, *123*
elk horn fern (*Platycerium bifurcatum*) 100, 102
English box (*Buxus sempervirens*) 43, 178
epiphyllum *104*, 106
Euphorbia spp. 42, *64–5*
'Black Bird' 18, 43
E. tirucalli see firesticks
Eveleigh Farmers' Market 145–6, *146*
evergreen magnolia (*Magnolia grandiflora*) 27, 43
'Little Gem' 18, 42

F

felt plant (*Kalanchoe beharensis*) 67, 73
fennel *132*
fertiliser 18, 136
Ficus lyrata see fiddle-leaf fig
Ficus macrophylla see Moreton Bay fig
Ficus pumila see creeping fig
fiddle-leaf fig (*Ficus lyrata*) 86, *86*, 116, *117*, 124, *125*
filler plants 43
firecracker plant (*Russelia equisetiformis*)
'Lemon Falls' 61
firesticks (*Euphorbia tirucalli*) 73, 84, 87, *87*, 110
flat-leaf parsley *132*, 133
formal gardens 12–43
fountain grass *see Pennisetum* spp.
frangipani (*Plumeria rubra* var. *acutifolia*) 50, *51*, 60, 116, 192
French lavender (*Lavandula dentata*) 122
furniture and accessories 118–19

G

Garden Life store 1, 171, *202–204*, 205, *206–209*
gardenia (*Gardenia augusta* 'Radicans') 50, 55, 60
Gardening Australia 143
garlic 140
gazania (*Gazania rigens*) 73
giant bird of paradise (*Strelitzia nicolai*) 50, *51*, *64–5*, *70*, 89, 106, *107*, *114*, 116, 122, *123*
giant mondo grass (*Ophiopogon jaburan*) 32, 43, 60, 86, 100, 106, *107*
giant pigface (*Carpobrotus acinaciformis*) 73
Goldsworthy, Andy 50, 189
grasses and grass-like plants 61, 73

green walls 102
groundcover plants 43, 73
Gymea lily (*Doryanthes excelsa*) 25, *25*, 27, 32, *33*, *40*, 42, 43, *58*, 79, 100, *100–1*, 182

H

Hall, Chris 197–8
Harvest: A Complete Australian Guide to the Edible Garden 143
Hibiscus tiliaceus see coastal hibiscus

I

ice plant (*Lampranthus aurantiacus*) 73, 76, *83*, 96
impatiens *see* New Guinea impatiens
India 189, 191
Indian hawthorn (*Rhaphiolepis indica*) 41, 55, *64–5*, 70
'Oriental Pearl' 61
'Snow Maiden' 37, 61
Iris germanica see bearded iris
ivory curl tree (*Buckinghamia celsissima*) 61
ivy *see* Boston ivy

J

jade *see* common jade; elephant bush
jade (*Portulacaria afra*) 43
James Street Reserve Community Garden 129, 152–63, *155*
Japanese box (*Buxus microphylla* var. *japonica*) 13, 16, *16*, 18, *20–1*, 26, *30–1*, 32, *33*, 37, 42, 43, 61, 84, 133, 178, 182
Japanese maple (*Acer palmatum*) 22, 60, 61
Japanese yew (*Taxus cuspidata*) 26
jasmine *see* star jasmine
Jerusalem artichokes 145
Juniperus chinensis see Chinese juniper

K

Kalanchoe spp.
K. beharensis 67, 73
K. orgyalis 'Copper Spoons' 42, 73, 77–8, 84, 96
K. tomentosa 82
kale 141
kentia palms (*Howea forsteriana*) 26, 89
kidney-weed (*Dichondra repens*) 87
Kurrawong Organic Farm 144–7

L

large spaces 10–87
Lavandula dentata see French lavender
'Leighton Green' conifer hedge 27
Lenti, Paola *119*
lettuce 133, *133*, 141
Levy, Sandra 77
lillypilly 13, 18, *20–1*, 26 *see also* weeping lillypilly
liquorice plant (*Helichrysum petiolare*) 61
'Limelight' 73
Liriope 'Evergreen Giant' 43
Lomandra longifolia 59, 73
'Tropic Belle' 55
Lunaganga *113*, 191, *192*, *193*

M

Magnolia grandiflora see evergreen magnolia
Mauritius hemp (*Furcraea foetida*) 42, 43, 73, 122, *123*, 177
Mexican bush sage (*Salvia leucantha*) 32, 55, *58*, 61
Mexican lily (*Beschorneria yuccoides*) 32, *33*, 43
Miscanthus sinensis 'Zebrinus' 61
mistletoe cactus (*Rhipsalis baccifera*) 87, *87*, 106, *111*, 178, 185
Modde, Paul and Gigi 178
mondo grass (*Ophiopogon japonicus*) 86
Moreton Bay fig (*Ficus macrophylla*) 50
morning glory *see* convolvulus
mother-in-law's tongue (*Sansevieria trifasciata*) 42, *107*
mounding plants 43, 61, 73
mulching 136–7
Murobond Bridge Paint 18, *19*, 110
murraya (*Murraya paniculata*) 43, 61
mustard greens *132*

N

New Guinea impatiens (*Impatiens* New Guinea Hybrids) 122
New Zealand flax (*Phormium tenax*) 42, 55, *58*, 60
'Platts Black' 77, 84
'Purpurea' 61
New Zealand rock lily (*Arthropodium cirratum*) 32, 43
Newtown courtyard garden 104–107

O

olive (*Olea europea*) 32, *40*
Organic Gardener 143
organic producers 144–9
ornamental grape (*Vitis vinifera*) 60
ornamental pear (*Pyrus calleryana*) 60
'Aristocrat', 'Capital' and 'Chanticleer' 43
outdoor furniture 118

P

Paddington courtyard garden 98–101
palms *30–1*
pandanus red edge or screw pine (*Pandanus utilis*) 70
peas 141
pencil tree *see* firesticks
Pennisetum spp. 73
Persian shield (*Strobilanthes gossypinus*) 37, *41*, 116
Philodendron 'Xanadu' 50
Pittosporum 'Miss Muffet' *see* dwarf Japanese pittosporum
Pittosporum tobira see dwarf Japanese pittosporum
planting times for vegetables 143
Plectranthus spp. 34
P. argentatus see silver spurflower
P. ciliatus 32, 43
plum pine (*Podocarpus elatus*) 133, 182
poa 73

Point Piper formal garden 12–27
ponytail palm (*Beaucarnea recurvata*) 88, *89*, 96
potatoes 141, *160*
pots and planters *119*, 124, *125*
    Dagar planters 37
    garden made of 76–87
    growing edible produce in 137–8
    hanging pots 102
    ideas for 84–87
    in Garden Life store 205
    Indian 201
    Italian urns *16*, 18
    recycled rubber *92*, *107*, *125*, 201, *201*
    Turkish *17*, *26–7*, *196*, 197, *198*, 200, *200*
    Vietnamese *125*, 201
potting mix 88, 137–8
Pratt, Philip *112*, 182

R
radishes 141, *160*
relaxed gardens 46–61
Rendall, Claire *121*, 122
repetition, creating 44–45
retaining walls 72
rhapis palm (*Rhapis excelsa*) 191
rhipsalis *111*, 178,*178*, 185
rhubarb *132*, *135*, *138*, 142, 161
rocket *132*, 133, 142
rooftop gardens 77, 93–7
Rose Bay rooftop garden 92–7
rosemary (*Rosmarinus officinalis*) 61, 73, 133–4
Rozelle garden 114–17
rush-leaf bird of paradise (*Strelitzia juncea*) *70*, 77–8, *79*, *83*, 84, *86*, 86, 96, *97*, *117*, 182

S
Salvia apiana see white sage
Salvia leucantha see Mexican bush sage
Savoy cabbage *149*
scale, creating 112–13
school gardens 165
Schultz, Richard *118*
screens
    Geo screens *63*, *67*, 106, *107*
    in vertical spaces 102
    jali screens *99*, 102, *103*, 110, *110*, 201, *201*

Newtown courtyard garden *103*, 106
Seddon, Richard *174*
shrub germander (*Teucrium fruticans*) 18, 25, *25*, *27*, 32, 37, *40*, *41*, 42, 43, 61
silver spurflower (*Plectranthus argentatus*) 43, 122, *123*
small spaces 90–125
snow peas 141
soil for vegetable gardens 134
sorrel *132*, 142
sotol 92
Spanish moss (*Tillandsia usneoides*) 100
Spartan juniper see Chinese juniper
spear lily (*Doryanthes palmeri*) 18, 55
spider lily (*Crinum pedunculatum*) 61
sponsorship for community gardens 167
Spring lunch 161–3
spring onion 142
Sri Lanka 188, *190*, 191–4
stag horn fern (*Platycerium superbum*) 102
star jasmine (*Trachelospermum jasminoides*) *24*, *26*, 43, 60, 100, 102, *102*
Stephanie Alexander's Kitchen Garden Program 129
Stephanie Alexander's Kitchen Garden Foundation 165
strawberries 142
Strelitzia juncea see rush-leaf bird of paradise
Strelitzia nicolai see giant bird of paradise
Strelitzia reginae see bird of paradise
succulents 23, 42, 78, *79*, 96, *103*, 119
suppliers 178–84
sweet bamboo (*Dendrocalamus asper* 'Hitam') 50
sweet violet (*Viola odorata*) 32
Sydney Sustainable Markets 146
symmetry 42, 88

T
texture, creating 74, *75*, *111*
The Edible Balcony 143
The Organic Guide to Edible Gardens 143
The Yates Garden Guide 143
Tillandsia usneoides see Spanish moss
tomatoes *137*, 142–3
travel 188–199
travertine 32, *40*, 63
tree aloe (*Aloe barberae*) 76, 84, 112
trees 43, 61, 73
tuckeroo (*Cupaniopsis anacardioides*) 73

tulip urns *123*, 201, *201*
Tumut Millet broom *134*
Turkey 197–9
Turkish tiles *98*
Twaddell, Graeme and Wendy 179
Twig café 157, 161

U
Unsworth, Mick 175, *175*
Unsworth, Richard (author) 1–3, 4–5, *4*, *153*, *155*, *167*, *174*, *182*, 189–99
urns see pots and planters

V
Vale, Nick 175, *175*
vegetable gardens 100, 132–43
vertical spaces 43, 102–3
viburnum (*Viburnum odoratissimum*) 32, *36*, *38–9*, 40
Vietnamese mint *132*, 137
Viola hederacea see Australian native violet
Viola odorata see sweet violet

W
Walsh Bay townhouse garden *45*, 108–11
warrigal greens pesto *160*, 161
Water lotus *193*
watering for vegetable gardens 137
weeping lillypilly (*Waterhousea floribunda*) 76, *77*, *83*, 87, *87*
Westringia fruticosa see coastal rosemary
Whale Beach garden 62–72
What to plant when 143
white flowering ice plant see ice plant
white frangipani see frangipani
white sage (*Salvia apiana*) 33
wild iris (*Dietes grandiflora*) 61
Wilkes, Annie 3, 5
Wollemi pine (*Wollemia nobilis*) 17, *17*, 18, 25, *25*, 26–7
worm farms 134–6, 138

Y
yoghurt pots 201, *201*
yucca 43

Z
zucchini *156*

LANTERN

UK | USA | Canada | Ireland | Australia
India | New Zealand | South Africa | China

Lantern is part of the Penguin Random House group of companies whose
addresses can be found at global.penguinrandomhouse.com.

First published by Penguin Group (Australia), 2014
This edition published by Lantern Australia, 2022

Text copyright © Richard Unsworth, 2014

Photography copyright © Nicholas Watt 2014,
except pages 3, 4, 54 (top), 78, 96, 106, 110, 136, 164–5, 189 (train and flower market),
196, 198–9: © Richard Unsworth
page 205: (café) © Georgina Reid
page 189: (Richard) © Michael Unsworth
page 139: beetroot © Anne Greenwood/Shutterstock; broad beans © Peter Baxter/Shutterstock
page 140: chilli © panda3800/Shutterstock; cucumber © Nataliya Ostapenko/Shutterstock;
garlic © Denis and Yulia Pogostins/Shutterstock
page 141: lettuce © asharkyu/Shutterstock

The moral right of the author has been asserted.

All rights reserved. No part of this publication may be reproduced, published, performed in public
or communicated to the public in any form or by any means without prior written permission
from Penguin Random House Australia Pty Ltd or its authorised licensees.

Designed by Daniel New © Penguin Group (Australia)
Typeset in Calluna by post Pre-press Group, Brisbane, Queensland
Colour separation by Splitting Image Colour Studio, Clayton, Victoria
Printed and bound in China

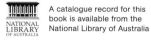

A catalogue record for this
book is available from the
National Library of Australia

ISBN 978 1 76104 885 2

penguin.com.au

We at Penguin Random House Australia acknowledge that Aboriginal and Torres Strait Islander
peoples are the first storytellers and Traditional Custodians of the land on which we live and work.
We honour Aboriginal and Torres Strait Islander peoples' continuous connection to Country, waters,
skies and communities. We celebrate Aboriginal and Torres Strait Islander stories, traditions and
living cultures; and we pay our respects to Elders past and present.